J. C. Vivian

Report of a Committee on the Royal Hospitals at Chelsea and Kilmainham

J. C. Vivian

Report of a Committee on the Royal Hospitals at Chelsea and Kilmainham

ISBN/EAN: 9783742816702

Manufactured in Europe, USA, Canada, Australia, Japa

Cover: Foto ©Thomas Meinert / pixelio.de

Manufactured and distributed by brebook publishing software
(www.brebook.com)

J. C. Vivian

Report of a Committee on the Royal Hospitals at Chelsea and Kilmainham

.

SECOND REPORT

OF A

COMMITTEE

ON THE

ROYAL HOSPITALS

AT

CHELSEA AND KILMAINHAM,

TOGETHER WITH

MINUTES OF EVIDENCE, &c.

Presented to both Houses of Parliament by Command of Her Majesty.

1871.

LONDON:
PRINTED FOR HER MAJESTY'S STATIONERY OFFICE,
BY HARRISON AND SONS,
PRINTERS IN ORDINARY TO HER MAJESTY.

1871.

[C.—275.]   *Price 7d.*

SECOND REPORT.

The Committee appointed by Minute of the Secretary of State for War, dated 10th February, 1870, " to inquire into the comparative advantages of In-door and Out-" door Pensions for the numbers who can be accommodated at Chelsea and Kilmainham, " and generally into the economy of the two Establishments," beg to submit the following Report, in continuation of that dated 5th July 1870, which contained the results of their Inquiry as regards the Royal Hospital at Chelsea.

Having visited Dublin and inspected the Royal Hospital at Kilmainham, and having obtained Evidence and Returns bearing on the subject of the Inquiry entrusted to us, we proceed to state shortly the main facts derivable therefrom.

The Royal Hospital at Kilmainham, for aged and maimed Officers and Soldiers discharged as unserviceable out of the Army serving in Ireland, was founded by Royal Charter of King Charles II. in 1679, and was opened in 1684.

The cost of the erection of the Building, which was placed on Land assigned by the Crown for the purpose, was £3,3591. 16s. 11½d., and this sum, as well as the cost of the maintenance of the Establishment up to 1794, was defrayed out of Funds derived from a deduction of 6d. in the pound from the pay of persons on the Military List in the Kingdom of Ireland. From 1794 until the present time the Establishment has been supported by Parliamentary Grants, aided by the Revenue belonging to the Institution.

The Parliamentary Grant in the Army Estimates for the year 1870-71 is 6,5481. 10s. 9d.; the Revenue of the Hospital, which is derived from the Rent of Land and other sources described in the Evidence, amounts to 402l. a year, and is applied in aid of the Parliamentary Grant.

The Land belonging to the Hospital was originally 64 acres, and its disposition is detailed in the Appendix.

The Hospital was constructed with a view to accommodate 300 In-Pensioners and the requisite Staff. This number was subsequently altered from time to time; thus in 1700 it was raised to 450, in 1729 it was reduced to 400, in 1838 to 300, and in 1851 to 140, which is the existing Establishment.

At the time of our visit the number of In-Pensioners was 139, one vacancy having recently occurred. Their Nationalities and Religions were as follow :—

English	..	..	..	7
Scotch	..	..	..	8
Irish	..	..	..	129
Roman Catholics	..	..	..	93
Episcopalians	..	..	..	43
Presbyterians	..	..	..	3

The admission to the In-Pension rests with the Governors, who are 23 in number, constituted as shown in the Evidence. A Board of Governors meets monthly to consider the cases of Candidates, which are previously examined by the Staff Officers of Pensioners and the Secretary, and by the latter submitted to the Board. A General Meeting of the Board is held about once a year, at which appointments to the Staff of the Hospital are made, and the proceedings of the Monthly Boards are reviewed and confirmed.

The following are the Qualifications for admission, prescribed by the Warrant of 1854, by which the Hospital is regulated :—

" The Candidate should not be less than 55 years of age, and have served 21 years " in the Infantry, or 24 years in the Cavalry, where the claim to admission is preferred " solely on account of age or long service. But in cases of the loss of one or more " limbs, or severe bodily wounds, or other injuries or disabilities, the result of foreign " service, disqualifying them for labour, the selection to be governed by the peculiar " circumstances of the case. Good character, both in the Service and since discharged, " to be an essential requisite; and preference should at all times be given to those men " who bear the best character, and have served the longest period."

A 2

No Candidate is admitted unless his Family (if he have one) is provided for; and, in selecting men, the Governors are mainly guided by the Age, Services, and state of health of the Candidates.

As is the case at Chelsea, we find that men are sometimes admitted to Kilmainham, who are below the age fixed by the Warrant, for the purpose of performing special duties, and of acting as servants to Officers; and that if a man ceases to perform such special duties, he is not necessarily discharged from the Hospital.

The average annual number of vacancies is 21. The average annual number of applications for admission and re-admission are 11 and 3 respectively, and the average annual numbers admitted and re-admitted are 22 and 3 respectively.

The average period of residence in the Hospital is about seven years.

The age of the oldest In-Pensioner at present is 87½, that of the youngest 30½, the average 63, and the average age on admission since 1st January, 1857, has been 68.

The average number annually dismissed, and the average number who have annually reverted to the Out-Pension at their own request, since 1st January, 1856, have been 3 and 6 respectively; and 4 have been sent to Lunatic Asylums during the same period.

The average annual number of deaths is 13, and the average age at death 83. During the period from 1st January, 1850, to 1st October, 1870, there was one case of suicide.

The rates of Out-Pension surrendered on admission, from 1st January, 1857, to 1st October, 1870, ranged between 2s. and 4d. a-day; and the following were the most numerous rates surrendered during that period:—

79	..	..	..	..	at 1s. a-day,
76	..	..	..	..	„ 6d. „
63	..	..	..	..	„ 9d. „

the average rate surrendered being 9d.

The average annual total Expenditure upon the Establishment for the period from 1st January, 1856, to 31st December, 1860, has been 9,543l. 18s. 2½d.; and deducting therefrom the amount of the Out-Pensions surrendered and other sums, as explained in the Appendix, the average annual actual Cost to the Public for 11 years has been 6,558l. 10s. 4½d., or an average per In-Pensioner of 2s. 6½d. a-day.

The average actual Cost to the Public of an In-Pensioner of Chelsea Hospital is 2s. 8½d. a-day. The larger expense at Kilmainham is accounted for by the fact that the Cost of the Secretary and his Clerk are included; whereas in calculating the cost of the Chelsea In-Pensioners, the Salaries, &c., of the Secretary and his Department are charged to the Out-Pension. Moreover, the larger number of Inmates at Chelsea naturally leads to a diminution in the proportionate Cost of the charges for Staff, Superintendence, &c.

The Warrant by which the numbers, duties, &c., of all connected with the Establishment are regulated, is dated 13th January, 1854, and the actual numbers of the present Staff and their Subordinates of all descriptions, are shown in the Appendix.

With respect to the Captains of Invalids, it appears that they only partially perform the duties assigned to them by the Warrant.

The Establishment of In-Pensioners, and the Staff, &c. connected therewith, occupy only a portion of the main Building, a considerable part of the accommodation being appropriated to Staff Officers of the Army and their Offices, and to the Offices and Stores belonging to two Out-Pension Districts.

The position of the Out-Pension Offices, &c. is stated to be inconvenient, and their removal to a more central position would be an advantage.

The Infirmary, which is a Building separate from the Hospital, contains accommodation for about 34 patients, and the average number of Inmates is from 26 to 20. Besides the Infirmary, a certain number of rooms in the Hospital Building are appropriated for the accommodation of the older and more feeble men, under the care of the Surgeon.

The Surgeon has drawn our attention to the difficulty experienced in obtaining eligible Nurses. Their pay at present is 1s. a day on appointment, and they receive one dress and apron a year. They are allowed fuel and light for an unfurnished room, but receive no rations or other allowances.

It is stated in the Evidence that no cases of complaint on any subject have occurred amongst the In-Pensioners, and the result of our Inspection was to convince us that the arrangements of the Hospital and Infirmary were throughout most satisfactory.

v

The condition of the men appeared to be one of complete contentment; and we noticed amongst them a greater appearance of domestic comfort, and of attachment to the Institution, than we had observed at Chelsea, a circumstance which may, perhaps, be owing, in some degree, to the arrangement by which the men are divided into parties of five, who live and mess together in one Room, whereas at Chelsea each man is practically isolated from his Comrades in a separate, and necessarily small, compartment.

Of the In-Pensioners whom we questioned on the subject, the majority expressed a preference for a residence in the Hospital to leaving it with increased pension, and one or two of them stated that they considered that 9s. or 10s. a day would not compensate them for the loss of the benefits received in the Institution.

On the other hand, the Staff Officer of Pensioners of the 1st Dublin Division, who has 1,004 Out-Pensioners in his District, stated that amongst this number there are many old and feeble men who are eligible for admission, but that they do not think much about the Institution, as they prefer to keep the command of their Pensions.

We have ascertained that there are about 15,000 Out-Pensioners in Ireland. Of this number there are about 1,300 who are between 55 and 60 years of age, and about 1,600 who are 60 years of age and upwards. About 2,000 have been rendered incapable of supplementing their Pensions by labour, in consequence of wounds or other disabilities contracted in and by the Service, and 76 are in Workhouses.

The number of applications for admission to Kilmainham is already always in excess of the number of vacancies, and we consider that there is no doubt that, if the advantages of the Institution were more generally known throughout the Country, the number of Candidates would be much more numerous than it now is. At present by far the greater proportion of applications come from Out-Pensioners in the Dublin District.

Having thus briefly recapitulated the leading features of the Evidence and Information we have obtained, we beg, in conclusion, to submit the following suggestions:—

1. We consider that the Captains of Invalids should (as recommended by us in the case of Chelsea Hospital) be considered as Inmates of the Hospital, rather than as part of the Executive Staff; and that in selecting Officers for these Berths, a preference should always be given to those suffering from wounds or other disability contracted in and by the Service.

2. We recommend that the minimum age for admission, except in cases of men admitted to perform special duties, or of men wounded or disabled in and by the Service, should be raised from 55° to 60.

3. We also, as in the case of Chelsea, consider that men who have been admitted for the performance of special duties, should, on their ceasing to perform such special duties, be discharged from the Hospital if still under the minimum age for admission.

4. In consideration of the heavy and incessant nature of the duties of the Surgeon, and the excellent manner in which these duties are performed by the Officer at present holding the appointment, we are of opinion that he should be allowed, when he has completed 20 years of Full-Pay Service, the Rank and Pay of a Surgeon-Major under the Medical Warrant.

5. We consider that the present emoluments of the Nurses are insufficient, and we recommend that they should (as at Chelsea) receive, free of charge, a half-Hospital ration, and also that they should be provided with furniture in their rooms.

6. The ordinary Ration of the In-Pensioners is in some respects larger in quantity than is necessary, and we are of opinion that alterations might with advantage be made by reducing the quantity of meat and bread, and by introducing a greater variety of dietary.

7. We also consider that the extra allowance to the men on special occasions, such as the Queen's Birthday, St. Patrick's Day, &c., should not be made as at present, by doubling their Rations, but by the issue of some special article of diet, or by a small allowance of money.

8. Though the Domestic character of the Establishment is not so decided as at Chelsea, we are of opinion that our recommendation in regard to the admission of the wives of some of the In-Pensioners into that Hospital is also applicable to the case of Kilmainham, whilst the structure of the Building is much better suited to such an arrangement than that at Chelsea.

---

* In the Committee's previous Report, on Chelsea Hospital, the minimum age was erroneously stated as 60 instead of 55.

9. Assuming that accommodation for the Officers, &c., of the two Out-Pension Districts is available elsewhere, we are prepared to recommend an increase in the number of Inmates. The additional accommodation which would be available if the Out-Pension Departments were removed would be equal to 40 single Quarters.

10. With a view to diminish the increased expense attending such addition to the number of Inmates, we are of opinion that reductions might be made in the Staff of the Hospital, and the present Staff of Adjutant, Quartermaster, Secretary, and his Clerk, appear to offer the means of making some reduction of expense. In connection with this recommendation we beg to draw attention to a Minute handed to the Committee by Lieutenant-General Sir W. Mansfield, G.C.B., Master of the Hospital, which is printed in the Appendix.

In conclusion, we would refer to the Return presented to Parliament on 26th May, 1854, containing "copies of papers respecting the proposed abolition of the In-Pension " of Kilmainham Hospital," which have an important bearing upon the subject referred to us.

We append a copy of a Warrant which has been brought to our notice since the date of our first Report, containing the authority for appropriating sums surrendered on sales of Commissions towards the cost of building the Royal Hospital at Chelsea. The amount derived from this source was about 1,800l., as shown in the Return (H) appended to our first Report.

Having now completed the duty entrusted to us, we would state that in our Reports we have limited ourselves generally to a statement of the results of our inquiry.

In the cases in which we have considered it desirable to offer suggestions involving alterations of the present arrangements of the two Establishments, we have not considered it within our province to enter into the details which would be required for giving effect to our suggestions, should they be adopted.

J. C. VIVIAN.

C. YORKE, General.

C. R. EGERTON, D.A.G.

C. TALBOT.

JOHN MILTON.

J. W. COARSE,
    Secretary.

War Office,
  24th January, 1871.

INDEX TO EVIDENCE.

MINUTES OF EVIDENCE

TAKEN BEFORE THE

COMMITTEE ON CHELSEA AND KILMAINHAM HOSPITALS,

AT

THE ROYAL HOSPITAL, KILMAINHAM.

Thursday, 20th October, 1870.

PRESENT:

The Hon. J. G. VIVIAN, M.P., in the Chair.

General Sir CHARLES YORKE, G.C.B.   Mr. TALBOT.
Colonel BRIDGES, D.A.G.   Mr. MULVY

GEORGE FREDERICK DOVE, Esq., examined.

1. (Chairman.) You are Secretary and Treasurer to Kilmainham Hospital be [...]?

2. How long have you held that office?—Since October 1864, having been previously, from March 1848, Clerk to the Secretary.

3. Will you be good enough to tell the Committee the origin of this Hospital, and how it was first endowed?—It was founded by Royal Charter in the 30th year of the reign of King Charles the Second (1679) (vide Appendix A). It is built on land formerly belonging to the Prior of Kilmainham, Chief of the Order of the Knights of Jerusalem. This land, [...] acres (Irish plantation measure), came to the Crown [...] the suppression of this Order in the reign of King Henry the Eighth. It was regranted by Queen Mary to one Sir Oswald Massinger by Letters Patent; but by an Act of the Second of Elizabeth the same was [...] to the Crown for ever, and confirmed to the Crown till King Charles the Second passed part of the lands, viz., 64 acres, for the use of this Hospital in Prior's Almnage for ever (vide Appendix B, C); the other part His Majesty granted in fee for ever to Sir John Temple, His Majesty's Solicitor-General, for valuable consideration. By His Majesty's Letter, dated 27th October, 1679, (vide Appendix D, E), "a dedication of 6d. in the 1l. was ordered " to be made from time to time out of all the pay " that shall grow due by the present or any future " Establishment to any person or persons whatsoever " upon our Military List in our said Kingdom (Ireland) " to be employed towards the building and erecting a " Hospital for such aged and maimed Officers and

" Soldiers as shall at any time be displaced out of our " Army as unserviceable men, and for making provi-" sion for their future maintenance." The Hospital was built and afterwards maintained out of the funds thus provided till the year 1704, when the deduction was put a stop to by the Government without any emolument for that purpose; and from that time to the present the Establishment has been supported by Parliamentary grants. The total sum expended in building the Hospital, Infirmary, Gardens, Churchyard Walls, &c., was 23,559l. 16s. 11½d. (vide Appendix F). The Hospital was opened in 1684. It was constructed with the view of accommodating 300 men, with other apartments and offices. His Majesty King George the Second, by Royal Charter, dated 11th April, in the 31st year of his reign, confirmed to the Governors of the Hospital and their [...] all lands, tenements, &c., granted to them by King Charles the Second (vide Appendix G). In the year 1709 the number of the pensioners appears to have been 450, the maximum. In the year 1729 the establishment was reduced, and did not vary, never exceeding 300. In 1833 it was reduced to 300, and in the year 1844, by Royal Warrant, it was further reduced to 140, its present [...] Establishment.

4. What are the sources of income of the Hospital? —The only private income is a rent of about 600l. per annum—derivable from rent of land let for grazing, 50l.; rent of land leased to War Office, &c. 13s.; interest on purchase money, Great Southern and Western Railway, 24l.; interest on 30l. to Government Debentures

Gen. F. Dunne. 30 Oct. 1868.

turns, and rent of fishery, 10*l*. Of the 64 acres granted to the Governors for the use of the Hospital, 21 acres 2 roods and 7 perches were conveyed to the Great Southern and Western Railway under an Act of Parliament some years ago. The purchase money, which amounted to 10,105*l*. 18*s*. is invested in the Government funds by the Court of Chancery, and the Governors receive half-yearly the interest, which amounts in the year to about 324*l*.

5. How is the total income of 462*l*. disposed of?—It is paid into the Bank of Ireland to the credit of the Governors, and it goes towards the reduction of the general expenses of the establishment.

6. (*Mr. Eliott.*) It is not expended in providing increased comforts to the men?—No.

7. (*Chairman.*) It goes in aid of the Parliamentary vote?—Yes.

8. You have stated that the Hospital was originally constructed for the accommodation of 300 men, and that in the year 1700 the number accommodated was 450. Was there any Royal Warrant or authority for that increase?—No. It was assumed in the first instance that the number of disabled men for whom accommodation would be required would not exceed 300, but it was found that the number increased. To counteract the Governors gradually augmented the Establishment, so that in the year 1703 there were 50 inmates. I find from the records there was not room for all those entitled to admission, and consequently a number of men were allowed out-pensions. That was the origin of the out-pension.

9. (*Mr. Talbot.*) Was any addition made to the building in consequence of the increased number of admissions?—No; but it appears from the history of the Hospital, written by the Assistant Master and Chaplain, that there were temporary buildings erected outside the Hospital about the year 1700 for the accommodation of the extra number admitted.

10. (*Chairman.*) Was there always a limitation that the men admitted to the Hospital should be Irishmen?—The Hospital was founded for the soldiers of the Army serving in Ireland. The Irish Army was a separate Establishment from the English Army at that time. It was for the Army on the Irish Establishment.

11. Not for men of Irish birth?—No; for men belonging to the Irish Army.

12. There were 450 pensioners in 1700?—Yes; and in 1789 the Establishment was reduced, and fixed at 400.

13. Was that by Warrant?—No, by the Order of the Governors, for which they had authority under the Charter.

14. Have they that authority now?—No, the number is fixed by the Royal Warrant of 1854.

15. In 1818 the number was reduced to 200. Was that by Royal Warrant?—No; that was by the order of the Secretary at War. In the year 1834 there was an attempt made to hand over these buildings to the Ordnance Department. That attempt was resisted by Sir Henry Vivian, the then Commander of the Forces here; there was a case submitted to the Law Officers of the Crown, who gave it as their opinion that the Governors could not hand over the buildings to the Ordnance Department without an Act of Parliament, and the matter fell through. Pending the question of the abolition of the Hospital, admissions were stopped; but in 1838 the Hospital was re-opened, and the number reduced to 200 by the Order of the Secretary at War or the Government. In the year 1854, by Royal Warrant, it was further reduced to 140.

16. What proceedings took place in Parliament between 1834 and 1854 with regard to this Hospital?—In the year 1834 the matter was not brought before Parliament, but a subsequent attempt was made to abolish the Hospital in 1833 when Mr. Shaw obtained an Order of the House of Commons to have all the correspondence that took place between Sir Hussey Vivian and the Irish Government and the Ordnance Office printed and laid before the House.

17. What action did the House of Commons take upon that?—The motion to abolish the hospital fell through. The Conservative Government or Party at the time, of which Mr. Shaw was a member, opposed it. Mr. Shaw being connected with Dublin, took a great interest in the Institution.

18. Consequent upon that motion, was any alteration made by the Government in the constitution of the hospital?—In the year 1854 the number of inpensioners was reduced to 140 by Royal Warrant.

19. Is that the first instance of any reduction or alteration in the Establishment being made by Royal Warrant?—No; there was a Royal Warrant in December 1845; it was something similar to the Warrant of 1854 (*vide Appendix H*).

20. Was it to reduce the number of in-pensioners?—No; it still left the number at 140, but it reduced some of the staff appointments.

21. (*Colonel Dyott.*) Was any reason put forward for the reduction in 1854?—At that time we could not keep up the number to 200.

22. (*General Sir Charles Yorke.*) You had not applications enough?—We had not applications enough.

23. (*Mr. Talbot.*) Was that the reason of the reduction in 1838?—Yes.

24. Not from any disinclination to vote money?—No.

25. (*Chairman.*) In 1854 the Royal Warrant fixed the Establishment at 140?—Yes.

26. And what Staff?—A greatly reduced Staff.

27. What was the Staff before the Warrant of 1854, and what was the reduced Staff under that Warrant?—By the Royal Warrant of 1818 there was a Master at a salary of 300*l*. a-year, and an allowance of 11*l*. a-year for his garden. He was also allowed furnished apartments, coach-house and stabling according to the number of horses, for which he was allowed forage, 30 tons of coals, and 200 lbs. of candles. Deputy-Master at a salary of 300*l*., who was also allowed furnished apartments, coach-house and stabling according to the number of horses for which he was allowed forage. The appointment was to be held jointly by the Deputy Adjutant-General and the Deputy Quartermaster General, each having a salary of 150*l*. a-year, making up the 300*l*. An Adjutant at a salary of 169*l*. 10*s*., with the usual allowance of quarters, coals, and candles. Four Captains of Invalids; the salaries of the four being calculated at 273*l*. 15*s*., in addition to their half pay; they were allowed also 10*l*. a-year each, to provide uniforms, with apartments, coals, and candles. The Secretary and Treasurer 300*l*. a-year, with apartments, coals, and candles. The Clerk to the Secretary and Treasurer 100*l*., apartments, coals, and candles. The Chaplain 250*l*., apartments, coals, and candles. The Physician and Surgeon 250*l*., apartments, coals, and candles. The Quartermaster and Steward 100*l*. 14*s*., apartments, coals, and candles. The Quartermaster-Serjeant 54*l*. 15*s*., apartments, coals, and candles. The Matron and Wardman 70*l*., apartments, coals, and candles. These are all the residentiary salaries. There was also an allowance of 629*l*. to the Governors, to cover the expense of nurses and washing, and an additional allowance to in-pensioners, for acting as lodge-keepers, and so on.

28. (*Mr. Eliott.*) There is no provision for this Establishment of 1845 for a Roman Catholic Chaplain?—No.

29. (*Chairman.*) The Establishment remained in that condition from 1845 to 1854?—Yes.

30. Under the Warrant of 1854 what is the Staff fixed at?—The Master's salary is nil, the Master being the Commander of the Forces; his allowance for garden is 100*l*. a-year, and he has furnished apartments, coach-house and stabling, and coals and candles. The Deputy-Master's salary is nil, he has furnished apartments, coach-house and stabling and coals and candles. There are two Captains of Invalids, whose salaries amount to 177*l*. 15*s*.; they are allowed 2*s*. 6*d*. a-day each, in addition to their half-pay of 7*s*. a-day. The Secretary and Treasurer has 300*l*.; the Chaplain, 200*l*., and a Roman Catholic Clergyman officiating to the pensioners, 50*l*. The latter is non-resident. The

Sir F. Dunne.
27 Oct. 1870.

Physician and Surgeon has 300*l.*; the Adjutant, 100*l.*, the Quartermaster and Steward, 100*l.*; the Clerk to the Secretary and Treasurer, 150*l.*; the Matron and Whitster, 40*l.*; the Quartermaster-Sergeant and Clerk to the Quartermaster and Steward, 64*l.* 18*s.* Eight Nurses, 173*l.* 7*s.* 6*d.*, with the addition in each case of apartments unfurnished, coals, and candles. There is an allowance of 250*l.* to the Commissioners or Governors, to cover the expense of employing in-pensioners in the performance of the duties of chapel clerk, watermen and scavenger, lodge-keepers, and so on.

31. That is to pay men for performing certain duties in the Hospital?—Yes.

32. An increase of pay, in short, to certain in-pensioners?—Yes, for duties performed in the Establishment.

33. (*Mr. Milton.*) The corresponding item in 1843 was 620*l.*?—Yes; but that included nurses and washing. The in-pensioners are not to exceed 140, viz., one serjeant-major at 2*s.* 6*d.* a-day; six company serjeants, at 6*d.* a-day; six corporals, at 4*d.* a-day; four drummers, at 3*d.* a-day, 10 privates, 1st class, at 2*d.* a-day; 20 privates, 2nd class, at 1½*d.* a-day, and 93 privates, 3rd class, at 1*d.* a-day—the whole amounting to 590*l.* 17*s.* 1*d.* per annum, to be victualled, lodged, and clothed according to the established rules of the house. These are the only persons who are victualled now; formerly the Captains of Invalids were also.

34. Is the Warrant of 1854 the last Warrant?—Yes.

35. By that Warrant the Establishment is now fixed?—It is.

36. Will you put in a copy of that Warrant? (*The same was handed in, vide Appendix I.*)

37. According to that Warrant the Chaplain is to have 200*l.*, but he is paid 250*l.*, is he not?—Yes; he was appointed before 1854.

38. He is at present receiving 250*l.*, but under the Warrant of 1854 his successor will receive only 200*l.*?—Yes; the other 50*l.* goes to the Roman Catholic Clergyman.

39. (*Chairman.*) Are you up to your Establishment now?—Yes; and have been for many years.

40. Is 140 men fill your hospital?—No.

41. What number could you accommodate in the Hospital?—There have been 400 accommodated in it.

42. (*Mr Milton.*) Without additional buildings?—Yes; many of the rooms are now occupied by Staff Officers and Offices; the out-pensioners' Establishment also has a number of rooms. Unless those rooms were vacated, I do not think you could accommodate more than 110.

43. A large proportion of the accommodation of the Hospital is appropriated to purposes not contemplated when it was founded?—It is.

44. You mean that there is not room for more pensioners than you have now, so long as a large proportion of the Hospital is appropriated to other purposes; but if all the accommodation of the Hospital were appropriated to the purpose for which it was originally provided, there would be room for 400 pensioners?—Yes, perhaps not for 400, having regard to modern sanitary improvements.

45. How many of the pensioners now in the Hospital are in the Infirmary?—By this morning's report, 37.

46. (*Mr. Talbot.*) How many would the Infirmary hold?—Between 30 and 40, I should think.

47. (*Chairman.*) What are the ages of the pensioners at present in the Hospital?—Between the ages of 30 and 40 there are 4 men; between 40 and 50, 10; between 50 and 60, 31; between 60 and 70, 34; between 70 and 80, 39; between 80 and 90, 11; total, 139. There were 140 on the 1st of the month; one man has been discharged since. The average age of the men at present in the house is 63 years. I have a return showing the ages on admission since 1851 (*vide Appendix J*).

48. What is the average number of applications which you have in the year?—I have a return, similar to that given in the case of Chelsea, showing from the 1st of January, 1848, to October 1870, the number of applications for admission to in-pension, the number admitted to in-pension, the number of applications for re-admission, and the number readmitted after having left. (*The same was handed in, vide Appendix K.*)

49. (*Colonel Egerton.*) What is the average number of vacancies in a year?—21. I have a Return showing the number of in-pensioners who have died from the 1st of January, 1850, to October 1870, showing the ages at which they died, from which it appears that the average number of deaths per annum is 13$\frac{5}{11}$, and the average age is 68$\frac{5}{11}$. (*The same was handed in, vide Appendix L.*)

50. What is the average number of discharges?—8$\frac{5}{11}$ per annum. I have a Return of the number of men discharged from the Hospital from the 1st of January, 1850, to October 1870. (*The same was handed in, vide Appendix M.*)

51. (*Chairman.*) What is the course of proceeding adopted when a man applies for admission into the Hospital?—When a man applies personally, he is first asked to produce his instruction papers and other documents. He is asked his regiment, rank, name, pension, age, service, foreign service, character on discharge, the cause of his discharge, his family, and how they are provided for, and the District in which he was last paid his pension. He is also asked if he has had any war service, and whether he has been wounded or has any Medals. This is all noted, and his papers are examined to see if they confirm his statement; his case is then referred to the Staff Officer of Pensioners in the building.

52. Are the cases of men not within his District referred to him?—I am speaking of men who reside within the Dublin District. I keep these distinct from applications from the country. I have here a form of queries sent to the Staff Officer of Pensioners (*handing in the same, vide Appendix N.*) The man receives a paper in which his name, Regiment, rate of pension, age, service, foreign service, and the cause of his discharge are entered, and he is desired to attend at the Infirmary the next morning and present that paper to the Physician and Surgeon, who examines him, and sends to me a Report as to his present state of health.

53. To whom does he make the application in the first instance?—To me. On applying to me he receives a form and goes with it to the Doctor, who examines him, and returns to me the paper accompanied with a Report as to the state of health of the man.

54. After that what happens?—I enter the Reports of the Staff Officer of Pensioners, and the Physician and Surgeon, and bring the case before the next meeting of Governors. A meeting of the Governors takes place once a month.

55. Supposing you had ten applications for admission to the Hospital, and there were only five vacancies, do you submit to the Governors of the Hospital the ten applications for them to select the men to fill up the five vacancies?—Yes, I submit them all, and from time to time they are re-submitted according as vacancies occur. When the men make a second application to me, I tell them that their names are retained on the list of applicants, and that their claims will be submitted from time to time as vacancies occur.

56. (*Mr. Milton.*) When the the list of applicants is laid before the Governors, do those who have applied first have the preference?—No, the Governors are guided in their selection by the man's service, and state of health.

57. I see in one case a man is returned as having a wife and three children. Are any enquiries made as to how the family is provided for in case he is admitted?—I find that he stated that two children were provided for by his wife's uncle. Unless that was confirmed by the wife's uncle, or the wife herself stated it, the man would not be admitted.

58. Is he called upon to prove that he has provided for his wife?—Yes, no man is admitted unless he can prove that he has provided for his wife.

59. (*Chairman.*) Is the amount of his pension considered?—The rules laid down by the Royal

Warrant of 1834, for the guidance of the Governors in admitting applicants are these:—"That each Candidate should not be less than 55 years of age, and "have served 21 years in the Infantry, or 24 years in "the Cavalry, where the claim to admission is preferred solely on account of age or long service; but "in cases of candidates applying on account of the "loss of one or more limbs, or severe bodily wounds, "or other injuries or disabilities, the result of foreign "service, disqualifying them from labour, the selection "to be governed by the peculiar circumstances of the "case, without reference to the period of service or "age of the applicant. Good character both in the "service and since discharged to be an essential "requisite."

60. Is there no limitation as to their being Irishmen by birth?—No, the fact of their residing and drawing their pension in Ireland is sufficient.

61. Have you in fact any Englishmen on the Establishment?—There are 7 Englishmen, 3 Scotchmen, and 163 Irishmen.

62. Were the 7 Englishmen and 3 Scotchmen resident in Ireland?—Yes.

63. You say the Governors meet once a month: are no applicants admitted during the interval?—No. Pensioners receive their pensions in advance; they have already been paid their pension up to the end of the month, so that they could not be admitted in the interval. They are selected at the Board Meeting for admission on the 1st of the following month.

64. What is the course followed with respect to applications from the Country Districts?—When I receive an application I acknowledge the receipt of it, and send a printed form to the Staff Officer of Pensioners to be filled up,—a form similar to that used at Chelsea. (*Form handed in, vide Appendix* O.)

65. (*Mr. Talbot.*) Is preference given to men who have large pensions?—Men who have large pensions have generally long service, and often wounds. The Governors frequently relieve men at 1s. a day because their claim is merely on account of age and service. Preference may be given to a man with 6d. a day pension, who is very old and has seen active service in the field.

66. (*Colonel Egerton.*) Preference is given to men disabled in the service?—Yes. In the printed form it is required to be stated whether the disability was the result of service.

67. (*Chairman.*) With the exception of your sending that form to the Staff Officer of Pensioners in the sub-district, the course followed with regard to applications for admission from the Country is the same as that followed with regard to applications from the Dublin District?—Yes.

68. (*Mr. M'[illegible].*) When men are admitted from the country, is any allowance made them for their expenses up to Dublin?—Yes; they get their expenses by Parliamentary train; there is an annual allowance of 15*l.* granted by War Office authority for that purpose.

69. (*Colonel Egerton.*) Do you take any means to inform country pensioners of the advantages of the Institution?—No; we have always had a number of men on our list in excess of our vacancies.

70. (*Chairman.*) How many men are there on the list now waiting for admission?—I think about 72.

71. (*Mr. Milton.*) By the Return you have handed in, it appears that during the last three years only half the number of applicants have been admitted, the number of applications being 191, and the number admitted being 87. Are not the remainder still on your list of applicants?—No; some of them have died; a great many have withdrawn their applications; and some are not eligible.

72. (*Chairman.*) How many vacancies are there at present?—Only one, which has occurred since the 1st of this month.

73. What is the age of the oldest man in the Hospital?—87 1/12, and the youngest 36 1/2.

74. What are the circumstances of the case of that young man?—He has always been in the Infirmary since his admission to the Hospital. It was a peculiar case. He was in consumption, and he had seen a good deal of service in the field.

Gen. F. [illegible]

29 Oct. 1872.

75. (*Mr. Milton.*) Can you produce any paper by which his admission is explained by the Governors?—The order of the Board is contained in this Register of the Proceedings of the Committee.

76. (*Chairman.*) When was the last Meeting of the Committee?—The last Monday of last month.

77. How many were present?—Colonel Armstrong, Colonel Nugent, and Colonel Fellowes.

78. What business was transacted?—The Minutes are not entered yet.

79. (*Colonel Egerton.*) Do not the Governors sign any warrant for the admission of a man to the hospital?—No; they merely order. The Governors' Order is marked on the list.

80. By the Secretary?—Yes; but the selection is made by the Governors. All applicants, except those who come from the Country, appear personally before the Governors.

81. (*Chairman.*) How many Governors of the Hospital are there?—23, 13 of whom are Acting Governors. The following were appointed by the Charter: The Lord-Lieutenant, the Lord Primate, the Lord Chancellor, the Archbishop of Dublin, the Duke of Ormond and his heirs male, the Chief Justice of the Queen's Bench, the Chief Justice of the Common Pleas, the Chief Baron of the Exchequer, the Secretary of State, the Master for the time being. These were the ex-officio Members; the Military Members appointed were the Colonel of the Guards, the Marshal of the Army, the Master of Ordnance, the Commissary of Horse, the Major-General of Foot of the Army, the Muster-General of the Army, the Captain of Yeomen of the Guard, the Captain of Troop of Guards, the Colonel of Regiment of the Guards, who were to continue as Governors so long as they continued in office. By the Charter it was provided "that the same "Governors and their successors shall for ever "stand incorporated to have a continuance for ever "by the name of the Governors of the Hospital of "King Charles the Second, &c., &c., and that by the "same name they may have a perpetual succession." The ex-officio Governors remain at the present time precisely the same, with the exception of the Duke of Ormond, whose title is extinct, and the Secretary of State, for whom is substituted the Chief Secretary for Ireland. With respect to the other Governors, according as they ceased to hold the appointments, successors to them were named. The first of these elections took place on the 8th of November, 1707, and they have since regularly continued till the present time. The present elected Governors are Major-General Newton, Commanding Dublin Garrison, Major-General Wardlaw, Commanding Cavalry Brigade; Colonel Armstrong, Deputy Adjutant-General, Colonel Egerton, Deputy Quartermaster-General; Colonel C. E. Ford, Commanding Royal Engineers; Colonel Budd, Inspecting Field Officer; Colonel C. L. Nugent, Deputy Judge Advocate; Colonel Radcliffe, Commanding Royal Artillery; Colonel Fellowes, Assistant Military Secretary; Lieutenant-Colonel St. George Nugent, Assistant Quartermaster-General; Lieutenant-Colonel Wynyard, Commandant Royal Hibernian Military School; and Captain Gordon, Brigade-Major. The Charter grants certain powers to the Governors. The following are Resolutions passed by a Board of Governors on the 28th of April, 1763:—"Resolved unanimously, that "the right of appointing a Reader, Deputy Reader, or "any other Officer of the Board is in the Governors "only, at a Board to be held for that purpose according to the directions of the Charter." "Resolved, "that by the above Resolution it is not meant to call "in question the power of the Master to nominate "any Officer upon a vacancy as a temporary provision "until a Board shall appoint." The Military Governors are the acting Governors; they meet once every month; once a month there is a Committee of Governors; the ex-officio Governors are all summoned when a General Board Meeting takes place.

Gen. P. Dunne.

29 Oct. 1872.

82. How often does a General Board Meeting take place?—About once a year.

83. What business is transacted at the General Board?—The appointment of Master, Deputy Master, or the Officers on the Staff; and at the Meeting of the General Board all the proceedings of the Committee are read.

84. Every proceeding is read and confirmed by the General Board?—Yes.

85. The ordinary Meetings take place every month?—The last Monday in every month.

86. What business is transacted at those meetings?—The tradesmen's accounts for the month's provisions, and all the expenses during the month are submitted, and the Governors sign Warrants and order the payment of those bills; besides correspondence also on a variety of subjects is brought before them.

87. And they admit pensioners and discharge pensioners?—Yes, and if any other business arises they transact it.

88. Have they anything to do with the out-pensioners?—No.

89. (*Colonel Sparrow.*) In what year was the awarding of out-pensions by the Governors of Kilmainham Hospital done away with?—At the opening of Netley Hospital.

90. (*Mr. Wilson.*) Was any diminution in the Secretary's office made when Netley Hospital was established?—No.

91. (*Mr. Talbot.*) What number constitutes a quorum at the meetings of the Governors?—Three of the Committee, seven of the Board.

92. (*Chairman.*) What has been the average attendance of the Members the last twelve months?—[illegible] at each meeting.

93. Have you any information to give the Committee with respect to the Master and Deputy-Master?—I have a memorandum relative to the appointments, compiled from the Records. The first Master was appointed by the Charter, and all successive Masters have been appointed by the Board of Governors, agreeably to the Charter. The Masters, until 1795, were appointed from "decayed Officers of the House." On the 12th of June, 1795, Lieutenant-General Sir John Burgoyne, Commander-in-Chief of Her Majesty's Forces in this Kingdom, was appointed Master; and since that time the Commander of the Forces has been appointed by the Board. With respect to the Deputy-Master; at first the appointment was temporary: he was merely appointed in the absence of the Master. On the 18th of May, 1760, the Governors "observing "that in the case of the absence of the Master, the "command and government of the Hospital must "devolve, according to the present Regulations, on one "of the decayed Officers who very possibly may not "be equal to such a trust," appointed an Officer second in command, with the title of Deputy-Master. On the 21st of June, 1792, Lieutenant-Colonel Pennefeather, the last decayed Officer of the House who was appointed Deputy-Master, resigned on account of ill-health, and "the Master proposed to the Governors Lieutenant-"Colonel George Hewitt, Adjutant-General, to succeed "Lieutenant-Colonel Pennefeather as Deputy-Master, and "that all succeeding Adjutant-Generals in the Kingdom "should hold the appointment of Deputy-Master." "The Governors were pleased to approve thereof." On the 27th of June, 1822, the Master proposed to the Board, "that as the Office of Adjutant-General had "not been filled up, the Deputy Adjutant-General for "the time being, should be Deputy-Master of the "Royal Hospital." "The Governors were pleased to "approve thereof." By the Royal Warrant of December 1843, the Deputy Adjutant General and Deputy Quartermaster-General were appointed joint Deputy-Masters. The Royal Warrants of 1843 and 1854 merely regulate the Establishment of officers, servants, and inmates, and do not interfere with the constitution of the Board, or their powers with regard to making appointments, in so far as they are in accordance with the provisions of the Warrants.

94. What is the average rate of out-pension surrendered by the present inmates of the establishment?—[illegible]

95. Have you a Return of the present Staff of Officers of the Hospital, including all the persons actually employed?—Yes. (*Handing in the same, vide Appendix F.*)

96. Have you a Return showing the number refused admission, and the grounds of refusal?—Yes; from the 1st January 1857 to 1st October 1872. (*The same was handed in, vide Appendix G.*)

97. What is the average period of residence in the Hospital?—Seven and a half years.

98. In considering a man's qualification for admission, do you consider the rate of out-pension he is receiving?—No; the Governors are guided entirely by the man's age, services, and state of health.

99. I mean, supposing one man is receiving an out-pension of 1*s.* 6*d.* a-day, and another man, a Waterloo soldier, is receiving 6*d.* a-day, would they admit the 6*d.* a day man in preference to the 1*s.* 6*d.* a-day man?—If the 1*s.* 6*d.* a day man was below the age of 55 they certainly would.

100. (*Mr. Wilson.*) In the case of one of these applicants I see the applicant states, "I was anxious "to get in, if only to get away from a worthless "drunken sister, whom I have been maintaining for "several years past" would that be considered a circumstance in his favour?—No; his claims were sufficient without that.

101. Then there is an application from a pensioner addressed evidently at the instigation of the Pensioner Authorities, for it is stamped "Refused Union," "As I am not able to earn a living (through) my affliction, I am most anxious to get into the old man's "house in Dublin," meaning Kilmainham. That is from James McKay; was he admitted?—He only applied this month. His case has not been before the Governors yet.

102. (*Colonel Sparrow.*) Do you think the Country Districts are fairly represented in the Hospital?—No; nearly all the applications come from Dublin. From January 1857 to December 1871, the number of applications from men in the Dublin Pension District was 575 (an average each year of nearly 38), the total number of applications being 950. The number at present in the house admitted from the Dublin District is 104.

103. You have told us that there are a certain number of men under the age of 55, the age mentioned by the Warrant; were any of those men admitted for the purpose of performing duties in the Hospital which older men could not perform?—Some, but very few.

104. How many men have been admitted into the Hospital for the purpose of performing duties in the Hospital?—Four; the waterman, the infirmary serjeant, the infirmary cook, and an Officer's servant.

105. Are those men now performing those duties?—The waterman, the infirmary serjeant, and the infirmary cook are; the servant is now Chapel Clerk.

106. When a man ceases to perform the duties for which he was admitted, is he still retained?—Yes.

107. Are there men now in the Hospital who were admitted to perform duties which they are no longer able to perform?—I only remember the case of the servant who is now Chapel Clerk.

108. (*Mr. Wilson.*) What were the circumstances of his case?—He was a young man who had a wound in the arm, and he was admitted to take charge of a Captain of the Establishment—to act as his servant—the Captain being almost helpless from paralysis. The Captain dismissed him and he is now Chapel clerk.

109. Why was he dismissed?—I do not know. Each of the Officers is allowed a soldier servant.

110. (*Mr. Talbot.*) The younger men are admitted as servants to the Officers?—No; some, if not all of those servants, are very old men.

111. (*Chairman.*) Do the men get extra pay for performing these duties?—No; their masters pay them what they like; they are relieved from attending any parade, I think.

112. What is the number of Roman Catholics in the Establishment, the number of Episcopalians, and the

number of Presbyterians?—There are 70 Roman Catholics, 43 Episcopalians, and 3 Presbyterians.

113. Where do the Roman Catholics attend service?—At the Chapel in James's Street, about half a mile from here.

114. (*Mr. Talbot.*) Does the Priest visit them during the week?—Yes.

115. And he attends at the Infirmary?—Yes, and gives them the rites of the Church, he or his Curates.

116. (*Chairman.*) Can you give us a Return of the rates of out-pension of men admitted into the Hospital since 1861?—Yes. (*The same was handed in, vide Appendix R.*)

117. The highest rate appears to be 2s.?—Yes; there is one man at 2s., the lowest is 4d. That was a "deferred" pension, and was the only case within my recollection in which, on reporting the man's admission to the Commissioners of Chelsea Hospital, they objected to the man's admission. However, upon a further representation to the Commissioners they did not insist upon his being turned out; though this man had only 4d. a day he had subsequently served in the Crimea under General McMurdo, and General McMurdo, who happened to be Chairman of the Board when the man appeared before the Commissioners for admission, remembered him very well.

118. Have the Commissioners of Chelsea Hospital a Veto on admissions to this Hospital?—No; they review the admissions; the Secretary for War has the Veto. Till that occurrence I always reported to the Secretary of State for War, merely sending to the Secretary of Chelsea Hospital the man's name, and the amount of his pension, but not the particulars of his case.

119. That was only to check the out-pension list?—Yes; since that time the War Office have requested me to send the particulars of the man's case to Chelsea Hospital, instead of to the Secretary of State for War, which has been done.

120. If an In-pensioner has any complaint to make, to whom does he make it?—I think the Adjutant will be better able to answer that. I believe he makes it through the Adjutant.

121. Are there any other details with regard to the admission of applicants, or with regard to the Establishment itself, which you would like to communicate to us?—I have made out several Returns similar to those which were furnished to the Committee in the case of Chelsea Hospital. I have a Return showing the charge upon the sum of 100*l.* granted to the Governor of Kilmainham Hospital to cover the expense of employing In-pensioners in various duties. The amount expended is 93*l.* 17*s.* I have accounted for the excess beyond the 100*l.* (*Included in Appendix F.*)

122. (*Mr. Milton.*) When do you make your Contracts for the provisions supplied to the Hospital?—Every six months. Tenders are advertised for, in three of the Dublin papers.

123. Have the prices of the Contracts been increasing the last few years, or are they less than they were before?—The prices have been higher; the prices of all provisions have increased very much of late years in Dublin.

124. How is the Clothing obtained?—By a Triennial Contract.

125. What is meant by the item in your estimate, "Maintenance of widows of soldiers"?—In the year 1823 there was a widows' fund established for the maintenance of a certain number of widows of the In-pensioners. That was an annual charge, but it has been gradually diminished. There is but one widow at present, and when she dies the charge will cease.

126. (*Chairman.*) Have you many married men in the Hospital?—The Adjutant has furnished me with a return of the number of In-pensioners who are married, and who have families outside the Hospital. (*The same was handed in, vide Appendix S.*)

127. (*Colonel Sperion.*) Are men admitted into the Hospital when they are in bad health, and then allowed to go out again after remaining in it for a time?—No.

128. (*Mr. Melton.*) How many men per year on the average have applied to revert to their out-pension?—Six.

Gen. F. Steele
29 Oct. 1870

129. On what ground have they made those applications?—The ground of the application never comes before me. The Adjutant sends in a form to me.

130. That is approved by the Governor without any reasons being stated by the man to the Governor?—Yes, if the man is not discharged for misconduct. When the man requests to be allowed to revert to his out-pension, his application is at once granted without any question.

131. (*Mr. Talbot.*) You say there are 63 Candidates on the list for admission. May we not presume that that number would have been largely increased if the accommodation had not been so much curtailed of late years?—I do not think so. There are, possibly, a great many men in the Country Districts who are not aware of the benefits of this Institution, and if we sent a circular round to the Staff Officers we would, no doubt, get a great number of applicants, but having as many as any list there is no necessity for doing so.

132. (*Mr. Milton.*) Have you many applications from Cork?—No.

133. (*Chairman.*) Will you furnish a Return showing the number of rooms occupied by others than the In-pensioners and Staff belonging to the Hospital. (*The same was handed in, vide Appendix T.*)

134. (*Mr. Milton.*) Are the In-pensioners permitted to send or take out any of their rations to their families?—There is no Order of the House against their taking out their rations.

135. Are their wives or children admitted into the hospital so that they can partake of those rations in the hospital?—Yes, there is no objection to that; but with the exception of the married men they are not allowed to carry their rations outside.

136. (*Chairman.*) With regard to the duties of the Staff, what are the duties of the two Captains of Invalids?—They are detailed in the Warrant.

137. Do they perform all those duties?—No; they are merely required to pay the men on Mondays; and in the event of any dispute between the Quartermaster and the Contractor with regard to provisions, the Captain is sent for to inspect the provisions. They also attend in the hall at the dinner hour.

138. (*Colonel Sperion.*) Can you hand in a Statement showing the war service of the men?—I have a Return of In-pensioners who are in possession of medals for war services (*handing in the same, vide Appendix U*). I have also a Return of the number of In-pensioners who have lost a leg or an arm (*handing in the same, vide Appendix V*).

139. (*Chairman.*) Have you a Statement showing the total expenditure on the Hospital from 1856–57 to 1869–70?—Yes (*handing in the same, vide Appendix W*); and I have another Statement showing the actual cost to the public of the In-pensioners of the Royal Hospital from 1856–57 to 1869–70, after deducting the pensions surrendered on admission, &c. (*handing it in, vide Appendix X*).

140. With regard to provisions, is a separate account kept for the Infirmary?—Yes; there is a separate dietary, and separate bills come in every month for the Infirmary. Those expenses are included in the column "provisions, clothing, medicines, and bedding."

141. Does your Return include maintenance of Buildings?—In the year 1848 the Board of Public Works in Ireland undertook the maintenance and repair of the Buildings, the expense of which had previously been defrayed by the Governors, under the superintendence of an Overseer of Works. Since 1854, the furniture, bedding, &c., for the men's rooms, and the furniture, &c., for the Master's and Deputy Master's apartments, have been supplied by the Board of Works, and for the last two years the Board has undertaken the supply of fuel and light. I have obtained from that Department a return showing the annual charge for those Services.

142. Does that apply entirely to quarters occupied by the In-pensioners, and by the Officers connected with the Hospital?—This is purely the Hospital account. I may be perhaps allowed to say that it is scarcely fair

Gen. J. Daunt. — 20 Oct. 1876.

to put the furniture of the Master and Deputy-Master as part of the expenses of the Institution, because if they were not supplied with apartments and furniture they would receive lodging allowance as Army Officers according to their Rank. The charge for "Maintenance, &c." also includes the expense of maintaining the Military Road which extends from the Hospital to the Railway Station, this road so far belongs to the Hospital that we prevent funerals and drays and wagons passing along it. The Building fell into disrepair, and the Board of Works have been gradually renewing it; that has increased their Estimates for the last few years; for instance, there are several rooms newly boarded every year, also several of the windows taken out and new ones put in, and other general repairs.

143. (*Mr. Milton.*) With regard to Contracts, when did the rise in price that you referred to take place? —Prices have been gradually rising the last ten years.

144. (*Chairman.*) Are you supplied with provisions from year to year by the same contractors?—No, we vary them considerably.

145. For how long do you make your Contracts?—For six months.

146. What is your meat Contract now?—7¼d. a lb. including chops for the Infirmary. I think the beef is without bone, but not the mutton. I believe the Contractor has to supply so many legs of mutton in the week.

147. (*Colonel Eyre.*) Did you find that the last Contract which you took was cheaper than the one you took previously?—No; I think about the same, if not dearer.

148. (*Mr. Milton.*) What special requirements are made with regard to your supply of meat?—Ox or heifer beef and wether mutton are supplied; and the following are extracts from the Particulars of the Contract:—

The beef and mutton for the Officers of the Establishment to be the prime parts of the carcase, and they are to have the privilege of choosing the joints.

The beef to be furnished for the Non-Commissioned Officers and Soldiers is to consist of the leg and round, hind quarter, without bone, skirt, or [illegible] ends.

Mutton for the Non-Commissioned Officers and Privates is to be delivered in the carcase, having the feet, head, and first joint of the neck cut off, and without suet or liver on the inside.

The meat to be examined by the Quartermaster upon delivery, who will have the power of rejecting the whole or any part thereof that shall be deemed of inferior quality, and of purchasing an equal quantity with that rejected, at the expense of the Contractor if not replaced by him within two hours after rejection; and in like manner to purchase, at the expense of the Contractor, any quantity of meat that he shall neglect to deliver by the space of twenty-four hours after it has been ordered.

149. (*Chairman.*) Have you any other Returns in hand in?—I have a memorandum relative to the Lands, accounting for the 64 acres (*handing in the same, vide Appendix Y.*) I have also a return showing the numbers in the Hospital on the 1st of January in each year (*handing in the same, vide Appendix Z*), and a return showing the pensioners fit for Hospital duty at the ages specified in the Return (*handing it in, vide Appendix A.A.*).

150. (*Mr. Talbot.*) Did I rightly understand you to say in answer to a question of mine, that if the accommodation in the House had not been curtailed there would not have been a great many more Candidates for admission?—If the number of the Establishment was increased from 140 we should very likely send circulars to the Staff Officers of Pensioners telling them that such was the case, and giving them a statement of the advantages of the Institution.

151. Would not the result of that be a largely increased number of applications?—We would receive a large number of applications no doubt from the country districts, where I do not believe the advantages of the Institution are generally known by the Pensioners.

152. (*Chairman.*) In short, you have more applications now than you can find room for?—Yes, from Dublin chiefly.

153. What are the duties of the Whitster?—To superintend the nurses, to see that they perform their duties, and also to superintend the washing in the Hospital. It was intended that the washing should be done by women in the Hospital, but it was found that it could be done much cheaper, and that it would entail less trouble upon the Institution, to have it done by Contract. We have a laundry building, and have made a Contract with a person to do the washing at 6½d. per week per man.

154. (*Mr. Milton.*) The Whitster has no duties now in the laundry?—She merely goes there and superintends the handing over the soiled linen to the laundress.

155. Is she chiefly employed as Head Nurse?—Yes.

156. (*Mr. Talbot.*) Does she receive the allowance provided for in the Warrant?—Yes.

157. (*Colonel Eyre.*) She really has substantial duties to perform?—She has.

(*Adjourned to to-morrow at 12 o'clock.*)

Friday, 21st October, 1876.

Present:

The Hon. J. C. Vivian, M.P., in the Chair.

General Sir Charles Yorke, G.C.B.	Mr. Talbot.
Colonel Eyre.	Mr. Milton.

Captain and Adjutant Wm. McGill examined.

Captain and Adjutant Wm. McGill. — 21 Oct. 1876.

158. (*Chairman.*) How long have you been Adjutant at Kilmainham?—Two years.

159. What are your duties?—I have to go down in the morning and mount the guard, to ascertain whether there are any prisoners, to receive any reports, if there are any, to communicate with the Commanding Officer in respect of dealing with defaulters, to parade the men at dinner every day, and see that all are present and rightly dressed, to parade them for church on Sunday, and maintain discipline as well as I can amongst them. In the event of any serious offence, such as drunkenness (of which I have known but few cases) I have to refer them to the Deputy-Master; but for any slight default, I am allowed to adjudicate the punishment myself, to give them three days in the Hall. I might give them six days, always communicating with the

Deputy-Master. In consequence of a representation made many years ago, that some of the old men were not able to eat their food all at times, they were allowed to take it to their room and eat it there, and the punishment is to make the man eat it in the Hall.

160. The man takes his own dinner away in his tin can?—Yes.

161. Those who are too old to fetch their dinner have it carried to them?—There are two or three whose dinners are carried to them—those are the men who are on the doctor's list.

162. What number of men mount guard?—We have only six who mount guard, and a non-commissioned officer. We have one sentry to prevent nuisances being committed, but in the event of the day being wet he is not obliged to go out. Another stands in the Hall to see that no irregularity is committed, so to take charge of prisoners if necessary.

163. During what hours of the day do they mount guard?—From 10 in the morning till 6 in the summer, and from 10 till 4 in the winter. We have no guard after that.

164. When do you parade the men?—At the dinner hour, and on Sunday for church. We have no further parade except on special occasions.

165. You say you have to see that the men are rightly dressed; how are they reported to be dressed?—From the 1st of May to the 1st of November (unless the Commanding Officer authorized the change earlier on account of severe weather) the red coat is worn; from the 1st of November to the 1st of May the blue coat is worn.

166. With a cap, the cocked hat being worn on grand occasions?—The cocked hat is never worn except on guard mounting, or at funerals. They do not go out in the cocked hat.

167. Do you parade the men for church in it?—No

168. You parade the men for church?—I parade the whole of the men at half-past 9, which is the time at which they have to go to the chapel. We have 93 Roman Catholics, but to make the parade all at one time we parade the whole, and then the Episcopalians fall out, after I have inspected them to see that they are properly dressed. The Roman Catholics march away, and the Episcopalians go to their rooms, and come into church of their own accord. In addition to the duties devolving upon me, which I have already mentioned, the duties assigned to the Captains of Invalids have to be performed by me, who from sickness or other causes they cannot perform themselves. These duties consist in inspecting the makers of the in-pensioners, visiting the men's rooms to ascertain that all is clean and regular, and to see the men paid their money weekly. The men living in the house are paid in the Hall, and those who are under medical treatment are paid in the Infirmary. At present one of the Captains is on leave, and the other is on the sick list.

169. Besides this guard-mounting, are there any special duties that any in-pensioners have to perform?—There is an orderly for the Quartermaster, and there are three drummers who mount as policemen, they are termed drummers, and have their pay so much—1d. a day instead of 1d.

170. What are their duties?—To prevent any unauthorized persons entering; to see that no one is prowling about the passages. There is rather a lot of men living in the vicinity of the Hospital, and these drummers are for the purpose of preventing petty thefts.

171. Are they on duty the whole day?—The greatest part of the day.

172. All these?—No; one every third day in turn.

173. Are they the sentries you find referred to?—No; they are in addition to the sentries. They are not confined to one place; they go round about.

174. Are they pensioners?—Yes.

175. What aged men are they?—One about 64, another 55, and the other between 60 and 70.

176. Was the youngest man brought in specially to perform the duties because he was a strong man?—I

do not think he was brought in specially for that purpose. He is one of

Captain and Adjutant
Wm. Neville.

21 Oct. 1876.

177. Besides the orderly to the Quartermaster, and the drummers, are there any men doing special duties who get special pay for doing those duties?—Yes, the following: men in charge of galleries, one charnel clerk, two messenger, one watchman, one hospital orderly, one Hall keeper, two cooks, three porters, two assistant cooks, one in charge of burial ground, one in charge of gas meters, one in charge of wine, one lamp-keeper, two barbers. Ten of the above are married and have their wives living near the Hospital.

178. These men are all pensioners?—Yes.

179. And all receiving extra pay?—Yes; receiving some varying from 3d to 1s. The drummers have 3d. instead of 1d.; the gate-keepers have 6d. extra pay; the cook in the kitchen has 6d.; the watchman has 1s.; and the chapel clerk has 1s.

180. When a man gets drunk, for instance, what do you do with him?—We should perhaps put him in the Hall. Offences are entered in a book.

181. (Mr. Vallad.) Have many been displaced for misconduct?—Some since I have been here.

182. What were they dismissed for?—One for assaulting the police; one for drunkenness and fifty inability—he was on tobacco, and should not have been in the place at all; another (who was a cripple and paralysed, having been by the infirmary all the time) was dismissed for being drunk three times within a fortnight; another sent was dismissed for calling his comrades; another for being absent 125 hours, which was six hours beyond the five days; another man (who was supposed to be insane, or feigning madness) was dismissed for insubordination; and another for insolence and disobedience of orders. That book will give the names of all those who have been expelled.

183. What is the average number of dismissals in the course of the year?—There has been more dismissed the last two years than for a long time before; I should think they did not exceed 3½; that would be about 17 in 5 years, but within the last two years there have been seven dismissed.

183a. What are generally the grounds upon which the in-pensioners apply to revert to the out-pension?—The reason usually assigned is that they "have got some light work outside"; sometimes that they "are going to their own place, to their friends." Of the latter class a considerable number apparently apply for re-admission to the Hospital. Upwards of two-thirds of the applications to leave the Hospital are given in between the months of April and September.

184. (Chairman.) At what time do the men get up, and at what time do they go to bed?—They get up at seven and go to bed at nine. The reveller is at eight, and they are supposed to be in at that time. Lights are out at ten in summer and at nine in winter.

185. What liberty do the men have with regard to going into the town?—Unless on duty, they are allowed to go into the town every morning after breakfast, which is at eight o'clock. Every man must be in at dinner or he is reported absent, and he must be in in the evening by nine in the summer, and by eight in the winter.

186. Except that they are required to be in at those hours, the men have perfect liberty?—Yes.

187. What leave you you give them?—I can give them leave till the following morning. If a man is absent beyond 12 o'clock, the next day I let the Commanding Officer know. It is very rarely that any leave is asked beyond 10 o'clock; they generally ask at dinner time for leave for an hour or two hours, and if there is nothing against them no objection is made to their having the leave.

188. Are the old men who have families allowed to take their partners out of the Hospital?—We have 14 men who have wives and families in the vicinity who are allowed to take their rations out.

189. (Mr. Mline.) In the ration larger than is necessary for the breath of the man himself?—Unless

Captain and Adjutant Wm. McGill.

21 Oct. 1870.

in the case of a strong man, I think it is more than an old man could expect.

190. Are any of them allowed to have their wives and families into the Hospital?—No objection is made to their wives visiting them, or their children.

191. When they so come to visit them, are they allowed to partake of the rations?—I do not know that that is ever done. If a man's wife or his child came and partook of his ration in his room, I do not think there would be any objection to it.

192. (*Colonel Egerton.*) Do you think there is no fear of the men selling their rations for drink when they take them out?—No. I do not think they would be likely to do that.

193. (*Chairman.*) If any of the pensioners have any complaints to make, I suppose they make them to you?—Yes.

194. Do you have many complaints?—Not many; sometimes the men make frivolous complaints against one another; some of the old fellows are childish, and they have quarrels with each other, and one complains to me that he has been abused by so and so.

195. Do you ever have any complaints of the discipline of the Hospital?—I never heard any.

196. Nor of the regulations?—No.

197. (*Mr Milton.*) Nor of the nature of the rations?—They sometimes say the mutton is very fat. I have never had a single complaint of anything of the kind.

198. (*Chairman.*) You think the men are contented and perfectly satisfied with their treatment in the Hospital?—I not only think so, but I am certain of it.

199. Do you think they would prefer remaining in the Hospital to going away with a small increase of out-pension?—I do not know about that; I think a great number would go anywhere for a little change if they had a little increase of pension, but I do not think it would be for their benefit.

200. Have you ever heard any of the men complain that this Hospital separates them from their wives and families?—No. We had a man come in the other day, having a wife and a daughter, who had 1s. 6d. a day pension. He is an old man of 88.

201. Where are his wife and daughter?—Near Carlow.

202. (*Mr Milton.*) How are they supported?—They have means of their own, I believe. He was a man requiring constant care; being an old and infirm man, I suppose he knew that he would get better attendance here than he would get outside.

203. (*Chairman.*) Is he in the Infirmary?—No, he is going about.

204. How many of the 130 now in the Hospital are fit for duty?—16 altogether, besides the non-commissioned officers. We have 8 serjeants, 8 corporals, 3 drummers, and 41 others.

205. The remainder being entirely unfit for duty?—I have not taken into account those beyond the age of 60, but there are many over the age of 60 who might be put on guard, or who might act as orderlies.

206. How many are bedridden?—We have on the average 21 in the Infirmary, and somewhere about 9 always on the flags, as we term it; men who can just move about, and are not fit for anything. There are 60 then we can never calculate upon being otherwise than having to be always cared for.

Lieutenant and Quartermaster JAMES WATSON, examined.

Lieut. and Quartermaster Jas. Watson.

21 Oct. 1870.

207. (*Chairman.*) You are Quartermaster of Kilmainham Hospital?—I am.

208. How many years have you been here?—Two years and seven months.

209. Will you tell the Committee what your duties are?—My duties are confined to the supply and issue of the provisions, the clothing, and the furniture.

210. What furniture?—The furniture of the men's rooms.

211. No other furniture except connected with the Establishment?—Only that.

212. The in-pensioners and the Captains?—No; the Captains have not furnished quarters; I have nothing to do with them.

213. You do not make the contracts?—No; I have nothing to do with the contracts except signing the bond after the contracts have been accepted.

214. You have to see that the meat is good, and so on?—Yes. I am every morning in the kitchen when the provisions are put in, and in the Hall at dinner hour.

215. It is your duty to see that the meat is of good quality?—Yes, and sufficient in quantity; and that the bread is good, and all the provisions.

216. Will you give us the cost of the clothing and the food of each pensioner, and the particulars of the clothing, the food, and the necessaries for each man?—I have here a Return giving those particulars (*handing it in, vide Appendix BB*).

217. Is the blue coat a great coat?—It was a great coat some years ago, but it has been converted into a frock coat. The blue jacket is a jacket with sleeves, of the same material as the body of the jacket which the men wear in the winter under the blue coat, and which they can wear in the summer as a fatigue jacket.

218. Do you ever have any complaints with regard to the clothing—as to the nature of the dress, or anything of that kind?—No.

219. Do the old men like it?—Yes. I never heard any complaints about the dress. I consider it a comfortable dress for an old man. Lately there has been some change proposed to be made in the dress, which the men appear to like very much. Some of the men have been fitting on the patterns, which has been approved of by the Governors, and which will be supplied in the next contract.

220. A change in the shape?—Yes. It is a more comfortable coat from being made double-breasted, of better material, and the style improved.

221. (*Colonel Egerton.*) Do you consider that the dress is sufficiently warm for any weather?—Quite; because in the summer they can leave the jacket off, and wear it under the coat in winter.

222. (*Mr. Milton.*) How is the bedding supplied?—By the Board of Works. When I find at the monthly inspection that any article wants renewing, I send a Return to the Governors, which is sent off to the Board of Works; and in place of all worn-out articles we get new ones. The Board of Works supply all the furniture, including the bedding.

223. (*Mr. Talbot.*) It seems that on Fridays the men have no meat. The 43 Church of England men and the three Presbyterians are treated in the same way in this respect as the 88 Roman Catholics?—Yes.

224. (*Mr. Milton.*) Do you ever change the tea for coffee?—Never.

225. (*Chairman.*) Do they get any soup on Friday?—No.

226. (*Colonel Egerton.*) Or any cheese?—No.

227. (*Mr. Talbot.*) Do they ever complain of this diet on Friday?—I have never heard them complain of it. The majority are Roman Catholics.

228. The others never complain?—I have never heard anything put forward as a complaint; but once or twice I have heard an old man say "the mutton is "too fat," and another reply "It is better to have fat "than have bones"; everything possible is done to suit them in this respect.

229. (*Colonel Egerton.*) You never vary the ration by giving bacon and cabbage instead of meat?—Never. They sometimes get bacon from the Doctor, for the Infirmary. I am sure the men would like bacon and cabbage occasionally.

230. (*Chairman.*) For the Infirmary there is a separate diet?—Yes. The Doctor orders the diet in the Infirmary, but I keep the accounts and check the bills furnished to the Secretary and Treasurer every month.

231. How is it supplied?—Through the Contractors who serve the House.

232. Are chickens supplied by contract?—Yes.

233. Did you never hear the men say that they would like a little more variety in the diet?—I never heard the slightest complaint about the rations since I have been here, still I am of opinion that a little change is necessary.

234. Do you not consider that the ration of 12 ounces of beef without bone is an excessive ration for the old men, considering that our soldiers only get 12 ounces with bone?—No, I do not think it is, but something might be taken off the bread and meat, and added by way of puddings occasionally.

235. (*Mr. Wilson.*) Some of the married men divide their rations with their wives, do they not?—That I could not answer. There are some married men who go outside to visit their families. I do not know that they divide their rations with their families.

236. They are allowed to take their rations outside, are they not?—I am not aware that it is done. I have never seen any order for it.

237. Is the 12 ounces of beef always boiled?—Always boiled. It is made soup of, and cut up in messes of eight.

238. And the soup and meat sent up in the tin together?—No; we have tureens for the soup, and the meat is served up in dishes, and the men at each table cut up their own.

239. (*Chairman.*) The beef is never roasted?—Never. Twice a week they have baked mutton, and meat baked in the improved cooking apparatus is considered to be equal to roast.

240. (*Mr. Wilson.*) Did you never hear the men say they would like the beef roasted for a change?—No.

241. On what occasions are they allowed extra rations?—On the Queen's birthday, on St. Patrick's day, and on Christmas day, they have a double ration.

242. On St. Patrick's day they have 24 ounces of meat?—Yes.

243. (*Colonel Sparrow.*) Do you think they turn some of that into whiskey?—I do not think they can well consume it all. I have often thought if the value of it were given in money to the old men, it would be a great deal more service to them.

244. (*Mr. Wilson.*) Do you think they would spend the money in drink?—A few might. To those who have families outside it would be of great service. A few might waste it in drink, but the majority would not. The cost of the extra ration is 1s. 0½d.; if they got a shilling it would be of a great deal more service to them.

245. (*Chairman.*) And you might exclude from it any man who had been drunk three times in the year?—Yes.

246. With regard to lights, how do you light the men's rooms?—With gas. There is one jet for each five men. Then they have the Hall to come into at night. That is lighted up and a large fire is kept in it.

247. Are there no other means of heating it?—No.

248. Are any amusements provided in the Hall for the men?—They have chess-boards, draught-boards, and four gaming tables.

249. Are the men allowed to smoke in the Hall?—They are; and spittoons are provided for them.

250. Do they use the Hall much?—They do, particularly in the cold weather. A good number were there last evening, some were sitting down, some were playing, and others were smoking.

251. (*Mr. Wilson.*) Is there any Library or Reading Room?—Yes; the Chaplain has charge of the Library.

252. (*Chairman.*) Do you think the men are generally satisfied with their treatment in this Hospital?—Very well satisfied. I have often heard men say when they have come in: "If I had known it was such a good place I would have applied long ago to come in." They did not seem to know that they would be so comfortable.

253. Do you believe that the pensioners in Ireland generally are not fully aware of the advantages of the Hospital?—That is my opinion.

Lieut. and Quartermaster Jas. Watson.

23 Oct. 1878.

254. Do you think if they were more fully aware of these advantages there would be more applications to enter?—I am sure there would.

255. Have you never heard the men complain that the arrangements of the Hospital separate them from their families?—No; I have never heard such complaints, but I believe that out-pensioners who are married and have families would apply to get in, who do not now apply, if they could live in the Hospital with their families.

256. You think that would be an improvement in the arrangements?—I think it would.

257. (*Mr. Wilson.*) Do you think that the families of any of the in-pensioners are in distress?—I believe not.

258. You have not heard of any distress among the families of the old men?—They have not any large families. One or two children would be the outside. When a man dies it is generally his wife, or his niece, or his nephew, who applies for his effects.

259. The Captains of Invalids have no rations allowed them?—No.

260. Nor are their rooms furnished for them?—No; they only get quarters, coals and candles. The Master and the Deputy-Master are the only Officers provided with furnished apartments.

261. Do you report when repairs are required?—Yes; I prepare an annual estimate which is furnished to the Governors, and they either send it forward or alter it.

262. (*Mr. Talbot.*) As regards the whole Building?—Yes; everything on the grounds belonging to the Hospital.

263. (*Chairman.*) Are there only two rooms in the Building appropriated to Aides-de-Camp?—That is all. There are generally two here, and they have two rooms each.

264. There are five rooms allotted to the Assistant Military Secretary for his quarters, and four rooms for his office?—Yes.

265. Five rooms are appropriated to the Staff Officers of pensioners?—Yes; on the ground floor, and three at the top of the house, making eight altogether. There are two Staff Officers of pensioners having four rooms each.

266. (*Mr. Wilson.*) How many clerks has the Assistant Military Secretary?

(*Mr. Dease.*) Four.

267. (*Colonel Sparrow.*) As to the nurses in the Hospital, are they rationed?—The nurses receive no rations.

268. (*Sir Charles Yorke.*) When a man dies in the Hospital you take charge of his effects?—Yes.

269. When a man is discharged, or goes away, do you take charge of his effects?—I do; a man going out would perhaps take his flannel vest and his cotton shirt, and so on, with him.

270. Do you see the clothing of those who die as well as of those who are discharged?—Yes; the men who come in wear the clothing of the man who has died or left the house. There is only one suit provided for the year. The greatest number of kits that I have had to take charge of, of men who have died or who have gone out, has been four; I have one at present.

271. (*Chairman.*) For how long do you make your contracts?—Six months.

272. (*Colonel Sparrow.*) Are the contracts made by tender?—They are advertised in the public papers, and tenders are sent in and accepted or rejected by the Board of Governors.

273. (*Chairman.*) When a man dies and leaves any effects you hand them over to his relations on their proving their title?—Yes; I take the papers to the Deputy-Master. Recently, when a man died leaving some money, we had to send to Donegal to get a certificate from the Resident Magistrate to prove that the person was what she represented herself to be, and we then sent over the money. When a man has friends in the vicinity he generally gives his things away before he dies, and then there is nothing left but the house kit.

374. (*Mr. Milton.*) When a man is discharged here is he provided with a suit of clothes?—If he has any of his own he puts them on, but in many cases the men have to take the house clothing, and then pay for it; they generally take their flannel vest and their prison shirt. Recently a man took his blue coat, for he had to either stand to wear.

375. (*Mr. Talbot.*) The cost of it being deducted from his pension?—Yes.

376. (*Colonel Sparrow.*) When a man is admitted into the Infirmary, does any one take charge of whatever effects or money he may have?—The doctor generally takes charge of the money; there is a place for locking up anything the men may have.

Dr. WILLIAM CAREY, continued.

377. (*Chairman.*) You are Physician and Surgeon to this hospital?—Yes.

378. How long have you been here?—12½ years.

379. Will you tell the Committee the state of the Infirmary?—To-day we have 30 men in the Infirmary; of these, eight men are bed ridden, two are acute cases, and the remainder chronic.

380. Is your Infirmary full?—No; it is not full. We have accommodation for three or four more in the Infirmary. Then, in addition to this, I have a certain number of rooms in the Hospital building.

381. Rooms appropriated to Hospital purposes?—Yes, for the more infirm men; they are called the doctor's rooms.

382. There has been no addition made to the Infirmary buildings?—Not since I have been here, except that the Infirmary Serjeant has had new quarters added.

383. What is the average number of men out of the 140 that you have under your charge, in the Infirmary and outside the Infirmary?—In the Infirmary the average number is 25 to 30; outside the Infirmary there are a great number of men whom I attend constantly, but the exact number I cannot say. Whenever a man wishes to see me he comes down; I encourage their coming down as much as possible. In the words called my words I should think there are about 50 men.

384. Who require daily attendance?—I cannot say that each man requires daily attendance. As a matter of course I may visit them, but they do not actually require it.

385. As to the diet of these under your care, do you make your own treatments?—No; treatments are made by the Board, but I order any diet I wish. I have a dietary which I drew up and which has been approved by the Governors; and that dietary I confine myself to as much as possible, but I have the power of varying it for any particular man.

386. You have a separate establishment?—Yes; the servants are kept separate.

387. What servants have you in the Infirmary?—I have one Serjeant, three female nurses, a messenger, and a cook.

388. Has the cook no assistant?—He has no assistant.

389. Will you hand in a copy of your dietary? (*The same was handed in, vide Appendix CC.*)

390. What is the nature of the complaints of the men in the Infirmary?—Almost altogether chronic, ordinary complaints, chest affections, and paralysis.

391. Have you no cases of fever?—Since I have been here I have only on one occasion had to treat fever; that was not among the pensioners, though it was in the grounds of the Hospital. We are wonderfully free from those kind of things. Even in the cholera epidemic, six years ago, we had but one case.

392. Have you any means of isolating patients?—I have a small ward for important cases of this Infirmary which has latterly been allotted for that purpose. I was trying to get it for many years; but it is so difficult to get the Board of Works to do anything. At last I got it.

393. Would that be a safe place in which to put a patient with a disease of a very infectious nature?—It would not be a very safe place. I would rather have the patient in an isolated building if possible.

394. Would you be afraid of putting a scarlet fever patient there?—I would not anticipate a case of

scarlet fever among these old men, but I would not like to put such a case there.

395. Are your duties confined to attendance on the men in Kilmainham Hospital entirely?—Entirely. I have no official duties outside the building.

396. I mean do you attend officially on those housed in the building and belonging to the Hospital?—No; these are officers, their families, and servants, about 20 in number, to whom I have at all times given my attendance, but I do not consider that I have anything to say to them; it is not part of my official duty to attend them. The Warrant lays down that I am to attend to the Invalid Establishment.

397. (*Mr. Milton.*) Including the two Captains of Invalids?—Yes; I also attend the Chamberlain of the Forces as Master, and the Adjutant-General as Deputy Master.

398. (*Mr. Talbot.*) Are you allowed private practice?—I do practise. I am not aware that there is any objection to it. I attend the majority of the Staff in Dublin at a nominal remuneration, just sufficient to cover my expenses.

399. (*Chairman.*) Have you a return of the number of men, out of the 140, in the Infirmary or out of the Infirmary who absolutely require constant medical attendance?—I have prepared that return (*handing it in, vide Appendix DD*).

400. Have you many ruptured men in the Hospital?—There are a great many ruptured men. I have no special return of them. Three men have lost legs, and one man has lost an arm.

401. Will you hand in a return of the number of men who are invalids from permanent disease, that with bladder affections, rupture, and so on, who will be invalids for the rest of their lives?—The annexed handed in, vide Appendix EE.

402. (*Mr. Milton.*) All matters connected with the health of the men and the sanitary state of the Hospital would come under your consideration?—Certainly; but many things are done affecting the sanitary state of the Hospital which I am not consulted about. The Board of Works carry out alterations without consulting me. I have recommended, and asked my Board to recommend.

403. The dietary of the men also comes under your consideration?—Yes.

404. You are aware that whilst the men have the question indeed, they never have the beef otherwise than boiled beef; are you aware of that.

405. Do you not think it would be an improvement if they had roast or baked beef occasionally by way of a change?—I think the diet might be very much improved, and after I had been here two years I recommended to our Board a change in the dietary.

406. When was the result of your recommendation with regard to the dietary?—The Governors agreed to give it a trial. I do not know what result they made; it was never tried.

407. (*Mr. Talbot.*) Did you ever renew that recommendation, finding it was not carried out?—No, I addressed a letter to Lord Sandon, the Master, on the subject, and intended to pressing it the Board to urge its adoption, but never renewed it again.

(*Mr. Dunn.*) This is the Resolution of the Board on that recommendation of Dr. Carey's. "The Governors "having attentively considered the above proposal of "the Physician and Surgeon, for a change in the "dietary of the Establishment, and having orally "examined Dr. Carey, the Adjutant, and some of the "inmates on the subject, approve of the proposed new "scale, provided it accords generally with the wishes of "the in-pensioners." The matter was never again brought before the Board.

308. (*Chairman to Dr. Curtis.*) Are the rations sufficient?—Quite.

309. (*Mr. M'Kean.*) More than sufficient?—I think they are, the bread, and probably the meat, might be reduced.

310. Each man has 12 ozs. of meat a-day without bone, whilst an effective soldier gets only 12 ozs. with bone?—These men do not care for so much meat, and on holidays they get double rations, which is a very absurd thing, for they make away with them. It would be better to give them 6d. or some little extra. They sell the extra rations now for 4d. or 5d.

311. Do not you think it would be better to give them plum pudding instead of 12 extra ounces of meat?—Yes. I understand that at Chelsea the men have bacon and cabbage one day in the week. Bacon is a thing the old men are very fond of.

312. Do you think the alterations which you suggested could be made in the diet without expensive alterations in the kitchen?—I do not think they would involve the slightest alteration in the kitchen. I suggested something in the shape of Irish stew on one day in the week, and plum pudding on Sundays. The men get a pint and a-half of "single x" porter. I recommended better "double xx" porter in reduced quantity.

313. (*Chairman.*) You think something might be taken off the meat ration?—Yes, off the meat, and off the bread, and added in other ways. Flour and little things of that kind might be given in substitution.

314. (*Colonel Egerton.*) Do you consider the Friday ration to be sufficient in bulk?—Yes; the lower orders in Ireland live almost entirely on bread. If the men were not in the Hospital they would be living outside on bread. The butter which they are allowed on Friday is a large quantity. I do not think they consume all of it.

315. (*Mr. M'Kean.*) Do you approve of the articles of diet?—Yes, they are very excellent.

316. With the exception of the porter?—That is very good of the kind.

317. (*Mr. Talbot.*) Are you allowed as much wine as you think requisite?—Yes; for the Infirmary. I think 100*l.* is allowed for medicaments and things of the kind, and that is quite sufficient.

318. (*Mr. M'Kean.*) In a sanitary point of view, do you think some improvements might be effected in the accommodation?—Yes; particularly as regards ventilation.

319. (*Chairman.*) Do the Clergymen, both Roman Catholic and Protestant, visit the infirm men in your Infirmary?—Yes, regularly. Whenever a man is seriously ill I let them know, and they attend immediately.

320. Without being sent for, do they visit the men periodically?—Yes.

321. Both of them?—The Protestant Clergyman attends almost daily, and on two days in the week to read prayers. The Roman Catholic Clergyman also attends very frequently.

322. (*Mr. Talbot.*) He lives on the spot?—Yes, the Protestant Clergyman.

323. Whereas the Roman Catholic Clergyman does not?—He lives in *James'* Street, within a short distance.

324. (*Mr. M'Kean.*) Do you report to the Director-General of the Army Medical Department in London on the sanitary condition of the Hospital?—I send in monthly sanitary reports and annual returns, and special reports in case of any infectious disease.

325. Does the Principal Medical Officer in Dublin consider it part of his duty to inspect this Establishment?—No.

326. (*Chairman.*) Who appoints the nurses?—The Governors.

327. On your recommendation?—Yes; that is, the nurses in the Infirmary. The other nurses are sent to me to see that they are physically fit for their duties.

328. (*Colonel Egerton.*) Are they all soldiers' widows?—By the Warrant they are to be soldiers' widows, if possible. Those in the Infirmary are. Dr. W. Curtis. 21 Oct. 1868.

329. Have they passed the examination to entitle them to superannuation?—I think two only have passed the examination.

(*Mr. Dunn.*) Two passed, and one or two did not pass.

(*Dr. Curtis.*) The pay these women get is very insufficient. It is impossible for them to feed and clothe themselves on 1*s.* a-day. They commence on 1*s.* a-day, and, as vacancies occur, they go up to 1*s.* 6*d.*, but they are for years on 1*s.* At Chelsea they commence on 1*s.* 6*d.* and get half rations. They have coals and candles allowed them.

330. (*Chairman.*) How do they get their food cooked?—They cook their own food in their rooms.

331. Are they allowed the use of the kitchen?—They might use it. They live on very little, principally on bread and tea.

332. (*Mr. M'Kean.*) You do not think they live on the rations of the sick men?—I do not think they can support themselves on 1*s.* a day.

333. Do not you think there is the danger that they are likely to supplement that small pay by taking part of the men's food?—There is that danger, but I am not aware that anything of the kind ever happens.

334. When fowl diet is ordered for a sick man, does he have half a chicken?—Yes.

335. The chickens are not very large, I suppose?—They are very good chickens.

336. Can a sick man eat half a large chicken a day?—Yes.

337. Do the nurses get any clothing?—Yes; they get one dress in the year and one apron.

338. They have apartments allowed them?—Yes, and I allow them to take a chair or other article of furniture when I can.

339. Have they no bedding allowed them?—They are not allowed bedding or furniture.

340. I presume you do not get such good nurses as you might do if the pay was higher?—No. I have the greatest difficulty in getting decent nurses. I find when a vacancy occurs it is the most difficult thing possible to get a woman to fill the vacancy; it is only by taking them on probation, and changing them constantly, that I can get anything like decent women.

341. (*Mr. Talbot.*) Have you made any representation to the Board upon the subject?—Not officially.

342. Are the women whom you get able-bodied and efficient?—There is only one young nurse—she is about 38; the others are old women. It is impossible to get young women for the situation.

343. (*Colonel Egerton.*) Do you think any increase of pension, within the bounds of any ordinary increase of pension that could be given to these men, would compensate them for the comforts and benefits which they get in this Institution?—It would be quite impossible. I have a great knowledge of people living about in the neighbourhood—pensioners particularly—and when they get ill they are in a wretched state and are robbed. It would be impossible to compensate them. In the House they have not only almost every comfort, but even I may say every luxury. They have wine, and even champagne when they need it.

344. (*Mr. M'Kean.*) Would the men prefer to go out on an increased pension?—Probably some would, but they would be in a wretched state. Men often come in starving, and in a short time you see a great improvement; they would be in the same state again if you sent them out.

345. If you sent them out, you would send them out with increased pensions?—A great many of them would not derive much advantage from the pension, because their friends or attendants would live on it.

346. (*Chairman.*) Some of the men would wish to go out, I presume, because the Hospital separates them from their families?—That is one very great reason why some of them would wish to go out.

347. If it were possible to apportion part of the

PRESENT.

The Hon. J. C. Vivian, M.P., in the Chair.

Gᴇɴᴇʀᴀʟ Sɪʀ Cʜᴀʀʟᴇs Yᴏʀᴋ, G.C.B.
Colonel Browne.

Mr. Talbot.
Mr. Milford.

The Rev. George Hans, examined.

376. How do you expend the 16*l*.?—In the purchase of books.

377. Do you expend any of it in periodicals?—Yes, we get the Sunday Magazine, but in volumes; we find when they are in numbers the men throw them about and do not like to read them.

378. Are any newspapers supplied?—There are paid for out of the monthly collections from the men and officers.

379. Over and above the 16*l*.?—Yes. The Library collection amounts to about 2*l*. 10*s*. to 3*l*. a quarter, half of which goes to the Librarian-Serjeant by order of the Board.

380. Do you think the men are happy and contented with their position in the Hospital?—I think very much so. I have had a great deal of intercourse with them. I meet them constantly in the Hall, and I never saw a better-conducted set of men, taking them on the whole, and they agree very well together.

381. (*Mr. Talbot.*) Are they generally a religious body of men?—The Roman Catholics I do not know anything about as regards their religious duties, but the Protestants, generally speaking, are very favourable towards religion, and very good men.

382. Do they read religious books much?—Sometimes; such as the Life of Hedley Vicars, and works of that kind. We do not get works of a controversial nature. There is supposed to be a Bible and Prayer Book in every room.

383. Do the Roman Catholics attend their Chapel in good numbers?—Yes, I think they all attend; they are very strict in their attendance upon their religious duties, but I have never interfered with them.

384. (*Chairman.*) Have you any suggestions to make to the Committee?—I think not. I think everything goes on regularly.

Rev. G. [illegible]
13 Oct. 1870.

Colonel R. B. Harris, examined.

385. (*Chairman.*) You are Staff Officer of Pensioners in this District?—Yes, one of them.

386. How many men are there in your District?—Chelsea Pensioners 1,004, Greenwich Pensioners 63, East India Company 117, Mercantile Marine 82, and Trinity House 1; making a total of 1,220. In the 2nd Division there are nearly 1,300.

387. Yours is the 1st Division?—Yes.

388. Among these 1,004 who are eligible for this Hospital, are there many old feeble men?—A great many.

389. What is the lowest rate of pension you are paying?—2*d*.; but there is only one of that rate.

390. He is not a Chelsea Pensioner?—No, he is an East India Company Pensioner, but he gets the 2*d*. for service as Store Clerk at the War Office.

391. (*Mr. Wilson.*) He also gets an Indian pension, does not he?—Yes, he does.

392. He draws that Indian pension from you?—He does.

393. (*Chairman.*) What is the highest pension you pay?—3*s*. a day.

394. Do you have many applications to come into this Hospital?—I think that there have been about ten this year; but it is not customary for the men to apply to me—they generally come to the Secretary. There is a little Form sent to me to fill up with regard to their character.

395. Do the men talk much about this Institution?—No. I do not think they do.

396. Do you think they look to it as a place they may come to when they are old men?—I cannot say they do. They are a very improvident lot generally. The pension I pay them on the 1st of the month does not go, as it ought to do, for their support during that month, but goes to the landlord, who has supported them for the previous month; the consequence is that they rarely see their pensions at all.

397. Your Offices are in this Building?—At present, and since 1813 or 1814.

398. And you pay the men here once a month?—Yes.

399. Are your Offices convenient?—They are very much out of the way.

400. Have not you applied lately for an increase of room?—Yes; we have other duties besides the payment of the Pensioners. I am Recruiting Officer, and I also enrol men for the Army Reserve Force. That has not been very troublesome hitherto, but I have sometimes thought that the chance of their being rejected when they come up here would deter a great many of them taking the trouble to come here. If I had an Office in a more central position it might serve both purposes as well, and be, perhaps, more convenient to the Pensioners when they come to receive their money. But there are a great many conveniences here too. We have a capital drill ground just outside the barrack gate, which was given over to us by the Secretary at War when he was here some years ago. Then we are very convenient to the Fort where we have our firing. There is a good parade ground here, all very essential matters where there are 400 (or more) men under arms.

401. Have you any Chelsea Pensioners in your District who are in the Workhouse?—Not many; I think I have, perhaps, four or five; one is a lunatic, two are very badly paralysed men. I think they generally run into the Poorhouse for the sake of the Infirmary.

402. Have some of these four or five men applied to you to come here?—One has.

403. The others have not, because they prefer to keep their pensions?—I think they like the command of their pensions.

404. In preference to coming into the Hospital?—Yes; at the same time I think it is a very injudicious notion of theirs.

405. (*Mr. Talbot.*) Has the case of the man who is in the Poorhouse, and who has applied to you to be admitted here, ever been laid before the Board?—I think he is on the list now, but he is a very helpless creature—very badly paralysed.

406. Therefore a fit subject for admission here?—I think so.

407. (*Colonel Spencer.*) Do you know if he has completed his service?—I believe he is eligible in that respect.

408. (*Mr. Talbot.*) How long has he been a candidate?—Upwards of a year.

(*Mr. Dent.*) He is a conditional pensioner, I think with short service, and a man who is not very old. The Governors have seen the man several times, and the short service and the age prevented them from admitting him. They admitted other Pensioners whose claims were greater.

409. (*Chairman, to Colonel Harris.*) Have you any discharged Greenwich Hospital Pensioners among your people?—No, not now. I had two; they were both very old men—upwards of 80.

410. Did you ever hear them talk about being sent out of Greenwich Hospital?—No, I do not think I ever did. There was one in the town and one at Balbriggan. The one at Balbriggan, though upwards of 80 years old, I believe, used to be continually crossing backwards and forwards between Balbriggan and Deptford. He came to Ireland because his wife was here, and he used to go back to Deptford because he had a clinging to the old neighbourhood.

411. (*Mr. Wilson.*) Do you think, if there were increased accommodation afforded, so as to give the means of admitting a greater number of men, there would be an increased number of applications for admission into the House?—I do not think there would.

412. Do you think the advantages of this House are sufficiently well known among Out-Pensioners?—They ought to be.

413. (*Mr. Talbot.*) Supposing an old Out-Pensioner

Colonel R. B. Harris.
20 Oct. 1870.

was receiving a very small pension, and was unable to provide for himself upon it, and was likely to go to the Poorhouse, would you think it your duty to suggest to him to apply for admission here?—Yes, I would.

414. Have you ever done so?—I do not remember having done so, but I think I would do so.

415. If you saw a man going to the Poorhouse, you would say why not apply to go into Kilmainham?—Yes.

416. (*Mr. Milton.*) Do your Pensioners who apply and fail to get admitted complain that it is a grievance that the place is not big enough to take them in?—No, I think not.

417. Is not a man disappointed when he sends in his name, and finds, time after time, that he cannot get in?—That is very often the case. This man I speak of, who was in the Royals, has been some time on the books.

418. Is he disappointed?—I think so.

419. Then there would be more contentment if there was more room?—Some of the Pensioners who have been admitted here, came not from the town, but from the country. Some of them have come even from England. They are transferred from an English district to me, and sometimes they are in the Hospital before their out-pension becomes due.

420. (*Colonel Egerton.*) I presume they are lonely men?—Yes.

421. (*Mr. Milton.*) Their application must have been sent to you according to the Rules?—Yes.

422. Do you think among your men there is a wish felt that admission into the House was more easy?—I do not think they care much about coming into the House, they so much like the command of their own money.

423. (*Mr. Tallot.*) Do you think they are fully aware of the advantages of the Institution?—Those in the neighbourhood are. A great number of Pensioners are paid in the immediate neighbourhood. They would learn the advantages of the Institution from the In-pensioners themselves. They have the means of informing themselves with regard to it.

424. (*Sir Charles Fox [illegible].*) In the Country Districts they have not the same opportunities of informing themselves, have they?—That is very likely.

(*Mr. Dunne.*) The case Colonel Harris refers to is that of Francis Quinn. Discharged 16th May, 1866, 28 years of age, 10 years and 3 months service, discharged for paralysis of right side, which occurred in India. Temporary pension 8*d.* a-day, which was afterwards made permanent at 8*d.*

(Adjourned.)

CONTENTS OF APPENDIX.

.D

APPENDIX.

(A.)

The Charter of the Hospital of King Charles II., near Dublin.

CHARLES THE SECOND by the Grace of God, of *England, Scotland, France, and Ireland,* King, Defender of the Faith, *&c.* To all to whom these Presents shall come, Greeting: WHEREAS We judging it fit and necessary, that some Provision should be made for such Officers and Soldiers of Our Army of *Ireland,* as by reason of their Age, Wounds, or other Infirmities, contracted in Our Service, are or shall become unfit to be any longer continued therein; and also unable otherwise to maintain themselves; We directed an HOSPITAL, to be erected near our City of *Dublin,* for the Reception and Entertainment of such antient, maimed, and infirm Officers and Soldiers; to the end, that such of the said Army, as have faithfully served, or hereafter shall faithfully serve Us, Our Heirs, or Successors, in the Strength and Vigour of their Youth, may in the Weakness, and Disaster, that their old Age, Wounds, or other Misfortunes may bring them into, find a comfortable Retreat, and a competent Maintenance therein. AND WHEREAS We of Our pious and charitable Inclinations, to so good a Work, have set apart and given Sixty-four Acres of Land, Plantation Measure, of Our own Demesne Lands, formerly enclosed in Our Park, called the *Phænix* Park, and being part of the Lands of *Kilmainham* in Our County of *Dublin,* and County of the City of *Dublin,* or one of them, for erecting the said HOSPITAL thereon, and for making fitting and convenient Walks and Gardens thereunto, and other Uses, for, and toward the support of the said HOSPITAL: The said Sixty-four Acres of Land being bounded on the East and South, with a Stone Wall, being formerly the said Park-Wall, and on the North, with the River *Liffy,* and on the West, with the Lands, being Part of the said Lands of *Kilmainham,* now belonging to *William Robinson,* Esq; from which the same are now divided, in Part thereof by a Ditch, and in other Part thereof by a Stone Wall, reaching from the Highway leading from *Dublin* to *Kilmainham,* to the River *Liffy.* And we have also named the Sum of Sixpence in the Pound for several Years last past, to be deducted out of the Pay of all Officers and Soldiers of Our said Army, and other Persons placed upon the Military List of Our Establishment, in Our said Kingdom, towards the Charge of building the said HOSPITAL, which hath hitherto been wholly employed therein. And we think it fit to have the said Deduction still continued towards the finishing the said Building, and providing such Utensils, Houshold stuff, and other Furniture as shall be necessary, or useful for the same; as also for the Maintenance of such Persons as shall be hereafter placed therein, until the said HOSPITAL shall, by the Charity of well-disposed Persons, or by some other ways, be provided of, and endowed with a sufficient Revenue in Lands for the Support thereof.

In order whereunto, we find it necessary to have a Corporation erected, to consist of such Persons in Succession for ever hereafter, as Governors of the said HOSPITAL, and may be enabled to purchase and hold such Lands, Tenements, and Hereditaments to them and their Successors, as may at any Time hereafter, be given to so good a Use.

KNOW YE THEREFORE, that We of Our special Grace, certain Knowledge, and mere Motion, by and with the Advice and Consent of Our Right Trusty, and Right Well-beloved Cousin and Counsellor, *Richard* Earl of *Arran,* Our Deputy of Our said Kingdom of *Ireland,* and according to the Tenor of Our several Letters, under Our Privy Signet, and Sign Manual: the one bearing date at Our Court at *Whitehall* the Eighteenth Day of *November,* and the other the Seventh Day of *January,* in the Five and Thirtieth Year of Our Reign, and in the Year of Our Lord, One Thousand Six Hundred and Eighty Three, now Enrolled in the Rolls of Our High Court of Chancery in Our said Kingdom of *Ireland:* HAVE ordained, declared, and established, and We do by these Presents, for Us, Our Heirs and Successors, ordain, declare, and establish, that the Building lately erected, and now standing upon the Lands of *Kilmainham,* on the South Side of the River *Liffy,* containing one large Quadrangle inclosed with a Stone-Wall, and all the Houses, Edifices, Buildings, Orchards, Gardens, Lands, Tenements, and Hereditaments within the same, and within the Site, Circuit, or Precinct thereof, or of the said Sixty-four Acres of Land above-mentioned, shall be from henceforth, and shall for ever hereafter continue and be an HOSPITAL in Deed and in Name, for the Receipt, Abiding, and Dwelling of such a Number of poor, aged, maimed and infirm Officers and Soldiers of the Army of Us, Our Heirs and Successors in Our Kingdom of *Ireland,* as shall by the Governors thereof hereafter mentioned, and their Successors, be named limited, or appointed to be lodged, harboured, abide, and be relieved therein; and also for the Dwelling and necessary Use, of one Master to govern all the Persons of in, or belonging to the said Hospital; and one Chaplain to instruct all the Persons that shall reside in the said HOSPITAL, in the Knowledge of GOD, and his Word, and of such other Officers as shall be found to be requisite, or necessary for the Use or Service of the said HOSPITAL; and that the same shall and may for ever hereafter be named and called, THE HOSPITAL of KING CHARLES THE SECOND, for antient and maimed Officers and Soldiers of the Army of *Ireland.*

AND FURTHER, We have granted, ordained declared, constituted, and appointed, and We do by these Presents, for Us, Our Heirs and Successors, grant, ordain, constitute, declare, and appoint, that the Lord Lieutenant, Lord Deputy, or other Chief Governor, or Governors of Our said Kingdom of Ireland, for the Time being; Michael Lord Arch-Bishop of Armagh, Primate and Metropolitan of Ireland, and Lord Chancellor of the same, and its Successors Arch-Bishops of Armagh, and all such as shall succeed after him to be Lord Chancellors or Lord Keepers of the Great Seal of Ireland, for and during the Time they shall continue in the same Office; Francis Lord Arch-Bishop of Dublin, and his Successors, Arch-Bishops there; James Duke of Ormond and such of the Heirs Males of the Body, to whom the Dukedom of Ormond shall successively descend or come; Richard Earl of Arran, Our now Lord Deputy of Our said Kingdom, and Colonel of Our Regiment of Guards there, and such as shall succeed after him, to be Colonels of the said Regiment of Guards, for and during the Time that they shall continue in the said Office; Arthur Lord Viscount Granard, Marshal of Our Army in Our said Kingdom of Ireland, and such as after him shall succeed to be Marshals of the Army there, for and during the Time they shall continue in the said Office; Francis Earl of Longford, Master of Our Ordnance, in Our said Kingdom of Ireland, and such as after him shall succeed to be Masters of the Ordnance there, during the time they shall continue in the said Office; Sir William Davis, Knight, Chief Justice of Our Court of King's Bench there, and his Successors, Chief Justices of the said Court there; John Keating, Esq., Chief Justice of Our Court of Common Pleas, and his Successors, Chief Justices of the said Court there; Henry Hene, Esq., Chief Baron of Our Court of Exchequer there, and his Successors, Chief Barons there; Sir John Davis, Knight, Secretary of State, and his Successors, Secretaries of State there; Gery Dillon, Esquire, Commissary General of the Horse of Our Army there, and such as after him shall succeed to be Commissaries General of the Horse of Our Army there, during the Time they shall continue in the said Office; Sir Thomas Newcomen, Knight, Major-General of the Foot of Our Army there, and such as shall succeed after him to be Major-General of the Foot of Our Army there, during all the Time they shall continue in the said Office; Abraham Yarner, Esq.; Muster-Master-General of Our Army there, and such as after him shall succeed to be Muster-Master-General of Our Army there, during the Time they shall continue in the said Office; Colonel Thomas Fairfax, Captain of the Yeomen of Our Guard in Our said Kingdom, and such as shall succeed after him to be Captain of the Yeomen of the Guard there, for and during the Time they shall continue in the said Office; Anthony Hungerford, Esq.; Captain of Our Troop of Guards there, and such as shall succeed after him, to be Captains of Our Troop of Horse Guards there, during the Time they shall continue in the said Office; Sir Charles Fielding, Knight, Lieutenant Colonel of Our Regiment of Guards there, and such as after him shall succeed to be Lieutenant Colonels of Our Regiment of Guards there, for and during the Time they shall continue in the said Office; Lieutenant Colonel Henry Brux, Quartermaster-General of the Horse of Our Army in Our said Kingdom of Ireland, and such as after him shall succeed to be Quarter-Master-General of Our Horse of Our Army there, during the Time they shall continue in the said Office; Major Rupert Billingsley, Major of Our Regiment of Guards there, and such as after him shall succeed to be Majors of Our Regiment of Guards there, for and during the Time they shall continue in the said Office; and the Master of the said HOSPITAL for the time being, shall and may be the Governors of the said HOSPITAL, and of the Members, Goods, Lands, Revenues, and Hereditaments of the same, at all Times hereafter for ever: And that the same Governors, and their Successors, shall for ever hereafter stand and be incorporated, established, and founded, in Name and in Deed, a Body Politick and Corporate, to have a Continuance for ever, by the Name of THE GOVERNORS OF THE HOSPITAL OF KING CHARLES THE SECOND, for maimed and unloved Officers and Soldiers of the Army of Ireland: And them the said Governors by the Name of, THE GOVERNORS OF THE HOSPITAL OF KING CHARLES THE SECOND, for maimed and unloved Officers and Soldiers of the Army of Ireland, into one Body Politick and Corporate, really and fully, for Us, Our Heirs, and Successors, WE DO erect, make, ordain, and create by these Presents; and that by the same Name they may have a perpetual Succession.

AND FURTHER, of Our like special Grace, certain Knowledge, and mere Motion, by and with the Advice and Consent aforesaid, We have given, granted, and confirmed, and by these Presents, for Us, Our Heirs and Successors, We do give, grant, and confirm to the said Governors of the said HOSPITAL, and their Successors, the said Site, Circuit, and Precinct of the said HOSPITAL, and the aforesaid Sixty-four Acres of Land, bounded as aforesaid, being Part of the said Lands of Kilmainham, and all the Houses, Buildings, Edifices, Orchards, and Gardens, that are, or shall be erected and made thereupon, TO HAVE AND TO HOLD, all and singular the Premises, together with their, and every of their Rights, Members, and Appurtenances, to them the said Governors of the said HOSPITAL, and their Successors, for ever: TO BE HELD of Us, Our Heirs and Successors, in Frank-Almoigne, without paying or performing any Rent, Duty, or Service to Us, Our Heirs or Successors, out, of, or for the same. And We do further, for Us, Our Heirs and Successors, grant to the said Governors of the said HOSPITAL, and their Successors, that the said Governors, and their Successors, shall and may for ever hereafter, Have, Hold, and Enjoy the said Site, Circuit, and Precinct of the said HOSPITAL, and the aforesaid 64 Acres of Land, bounded as aforesaid, being Part of the said Lands of Kilmainham; and all the Houses, Buildings, Edifices, Orchards, and Gardens, that are, or shall be erected, or made thereupon; and all the Householdments, Furniture, Plate, Money, Revenues, Goods, and Chattels, that have been, or shall be given unto or purchased, for the Use of the said HOSPITAL, or of the Persons residing, or to reside therein, or belonging, or that shall hereafter belong thereunto; and that by the same Name of, GOVERNORS OF THE HOSPITAL OF KING CHARLES THE SECOND, for maimed and unloved Officers and Soldiers of the Army of Ireland, they be, and shall be for ever, Persons able and capable in Law, to Have, Take, Purchase, Hold, Receive, Possess, and Enjoy, as well any Manors, Lands, Tenements, Liberties, Franchises, Rents, Reversions, Privileges, and other Hereditaments, in Fee to them, and their Successors for ever, to the Value of Six Thousand

Pounds per Ann. (notwithstanding the Statute of Quia Emptores Terrarum, or any other Statute, to the contrary) As also all and singular, Courts, Castles, and other Things whatsoever, and the same Lands, Tenements, and Hereditaments, and every or any of them (other than the said Hospital-House, and the Out-Houses, Orchards, Gardens, Walks, and Back-sides, that are, or shall be set apart or used, for the Habitation, or Use of the Master, Chaplain, Soldiers, or Officers, or Attendants of the said Hospital, or any of them) to demise, set and let, for the Term of Thirty-one Years or under, in Possession and not in Reversion, or for One, Two, or Three Lives, or for any Number of Years determinable upon One, Two, or Three Lives in Possession, and not in Reversion: and whereupon such yearly Rent, or more shall be reserved, to the said Governor of the said Hospital and their Successors, during the Continuance of every such Lease, as at the Time of making such Lease, shall have been reserved upon any Demise thereof, or otherwise, at the true yearly Value thereof: And to Seal and Execute all Deeds, Evidences, and Writings, of, in, and concerning the same, and every Parcel thereof, in the behalf needful or convenient to be had or made; and by the same Name of, GOVERNORS OF THE HOSPITAL OF KING CHARLES THE SECOND, for entire and use and Soldiers of the Army of Ireland, they shall and may be Persons able and capable in Law, to plead and be impleaded, answer and be answered, defend and be defended, in any Our Courts, and other Places whatsoever, and before any Judge, Judges, Justices, or any other Person or Persons whatsoever, in all and all manner of Suits, Complaints, Pleas, Causes, Matters, and Demands, of whatsoever Kind, Nature, or Form they be, in the same Manner and Form as others of Our Liege People, of this Our Realm of Ireland, being Persons able and capable in Law, may implead and be impleaded, answer and be answered, defend or be defended or may Have, Purchase, Receive, Take, Possess, or Enjoy any Lands, Tenements, or Hereditaments, or Goods, or Chattels, by any lawful Ways or Means whatsoever. And also, that the said Governors of the said Hospital, and their Successors, shall and may have, and use for ever, a Common Seal, for them and their Successors, to serve for the Ensealing, Making and Executing such Demises, Leases, Deeds, and other Things, Matters, and Affairs, touching, in or any wise concerning the said Incorporation, with such a Stamp, and Inscription, to be ingraven and made therein, as to the said Governors, or the major part of them, shall be thought fit; and that it shall and may be lawful to and for the said Governors, and their Successors, the same Seal, at their Will and Pleasure, from Time to Time, to break, deface, alter, and make new, as to them, or the major part of them, shall seem meet, fit, and expedient. The said Common Seal to remain in the Custody of such Person or Persons, as the said Governors, or the major part of them shall think fit; but not to be affixed to any Deed, Writing, or other Instrument, without the Consent of the said Governors, or the major part of them, under their Hands thereunto first had and obtained.

AND FURTHER, of Our special Grace, certain Knowledge, and meer Motion, by and with the Advice and Consent aforesaid, We Will, and by these Presents, for Us, Our Heirs and Successors, We do grant, that from henceforth for ever there be, and shall be One Master of the said Hospital, and also one Chaplain, and such other Officers, in, and belonging to the said Hospital, as the said Governors or the major part of them, shall think fit and necessary to appoint for the Service thereof; And for the good Rule and Government of the said Hospital, We have assigned, named, ordained, and constituted, and by these Presents for Us, Our Heirs and Successors, do assign, name, ordain, and constitute, Our Trusty and Well-beloved, John Jeffreys Esq; to be the First Master of the said Hospital, willing that the said John Jeffreys be and continue Master of the said Hospital, during his good Behaviour to the said Hospital; and that all succeeding Masters of the said Hospital, and the First Chaplain thereof, and his Successors, and all such other Officers as shall be thought fit by the said Governors of the said Hospital or the major part of them, to be appointed for the Service thereof, be chosen and constituted by the said Governors, or the major part of them, by Instrument under their Hands and Common Seal. And that the said John Jeffreys, and all succeeding Masters of the said Hospital, and the said Chaplain, and all other Officers, in or relating to the said Hospital, shall take the Oaths of Allegiance and Supremacy; and also such an Oath, for the due Execution of their respective Office, as by the Governors of the said Hospital, or the major part of them, shall be set down and prescribed before the Governors of the said Hospital, or any three of them, whom We do Impower and Authorise, to Administer the said Oaths, before they or any of them do enter upon the Execution of the said respective Offices; and that the said Master, Chaplain, and other Officers have such Fees, Salaries, and Allowances out of the Revenues of the said Hospital, for and towards their respective Support and Maintenance, as by the said Governors, or the major part of them, shall be thought fit to be Granted, Assigned, or Allowed to them; and shall also Observe and Perform all such Rules, Orders, and Directions, in or relating to the due Execution of their said respective Offices, as by the said Governors, or the major part of them, shall be from Time to Time agreed on, Ordered, and Prescribed, to, or for them respectively: and shall also be subject and liable upon any Neglect or Misearriage in their respective Offices and Employments, to be Removed, Displaced, and Suspended from the Execution of their said respective Offices, by the said Governors, or the major part of them, who are hereby also impowered thereupon, to put others in their respective Places, in such manner as they shall think fit.

AND OUR further Will and Pleasure is, and We do hereby Grant and Declare, That whensoever the said Office, or Place of Master of the said Hospital shall next become Vacant, no Person shall be chosen Master of the said Hospital, but such a Person as shall be of the Protestant Religion, as by Law established in the Church of Ireland, and a Gentleman by Descent, and of above Fifty Years of Age, and an unmarried Man, and one that hath served Our Royal Father, or Us, or shall have served Us, Our Heirs or Successors in the Army of Us, Our Heirs or Successors in the Army of Ireland in the capacity of a Captain at least, and shall have been of the said Army, for the space of Ten Years, and never have Arms against Us or any of Our Predecessors, and that shall not have, of his own Estate, to the value of One Hundred Pounds per Annum, at the Time of his Election, and who shall then immediately quit his Command in the Army (if any he shall then have in the said Army;) but if an acting Person shall be found to be chosen Master of the said Hospital, who shall have all the said Qualifications; then and in such Case the said Governors, or the major part of them, shall choose such a fit Person as they shall think fit, who shall have as many of the said Qualifications, as they, or the major part of them can find to any Person, who shall be by them judged to be fit for the said Office, But if no Person shall be chosen by them to be Master of the said Hospital within two Months after the said Office of Master of the said Hospital shall hereafter become Vacant; That then and in every such Case, it shall and may be lawful to and for the Lord Lieutenant, Lord Deputy, or other chief Governor or Governors of Our said Realm of Ireland, by any Writing under his Hand, to Nominate and Appoint some such meet and fitting Person, as is herein abovementioned, to the said Office of Master of the said Hospital, that shall be so void by such Default of the said Governors and their Successors for the term being, or the major part of them, as aforesaid, with such Qualifications as are mentioned for him to have, in Case he had been chosen by the Governors of the Hospital; or if no fit Person can be found with all the said Qualifications, then to appoint one with as many of them as he shall find in any Person, fit for the said place.

AND FURTHER, Our Will and Pleasure is, and We do hereby for Us, Our Heirs and Successors, Grant, Ordain, and Declare, that the Master of the said Hospital shall have the Military and Civil Government of the said Hospital, and shall have Power to Administer an Oath to any Person or Persons, in any Cause relating to the Affairs of the said Hospital, or any the Officers or Members thereof. And also that upon every Vacancy of the said Office of Master of the said Hospital, whether by Death, Deprivation, Resignation, or otherwise, the Government of the said Hospital, during such Vacancy, and until a new Master shall be chosen or appointed, shall devolve on the next Military Officer residing in the said Hospital, according to the Dignity and Priority of his Commission, who shall govern the Affairs of the said Hospital in all such Matters as shall be necessary to be done, during such Vacancy, and cannot without Prejudice be deferred until the Appointment of a new Master thereof. And also that the Master of the said Hospital shall constantly inhabit and reside in the Lodgings appointed for him in the said Hospital, and shall Eat constantly in the common Hall there, at a Table to be provided for himself, (except in Case of Sickness, or other just Occasion) together with the Chaplain, and such Gentlemen of the said Hospital, as shall have been One or Our Successors Commission, and such other Officers of the said Hospital, as he shall admit thereunto; and shall not be absent from the said Hospital, above the space of one Month, in any Year, without the Licence of the said Governors, or the major part of them under their Hands, and shall have Power and Authority, by Writing under his Hand and Seal, to depute and appoint some commissioned Officer residing within the said Hospital to be Deputy-Master thereof, during such his absence from the same.

AND FURTHER, Our Will and Pleasure is, and We do hereby for Us, Our Heirs and Successors, Grant, Ordain, Declare and Appoint, that the said Governors and their Successors for the time being, or the major part of them, shall have full Power and Authority to do, perform, and execute, all and every such lawful Acts and Things, good, necessary, and profitable for the said Hospital, and the several Persons therein, to be from time to time, placed in at large, full and ample manner and form, to all intents, constructions, and purposes, as any other Body Politick or Corporate, in Our Kingdoms of England or Ireland, fully and perfectly founded and incorporated, may do; and shall and may have full Power and Authority to nominate and appoint, when and as often as they shall think good, such a Number of Officers and Soldiers of the said Army, who during their continuance therein, have been or shall be maimed; or who having served Seven Years at least in the said Army, have been or shall become Aged, Infirm, or Unserviceable, to be placed, lodged, and maintained in the said Hospital, as the Lodging and Revenue of the said Hospital shall hold out, to maintain and provide for, and to appoint, increase, and lessen their Number and their Salaries, and Allowances; as also the respective Allowances and Salaries of the said Master, Chaplain, and other Officers and Servants of the said Hospital, accordingly, as the Revenue of the said Hospital shall from Time to Time lessen or increase, or otherwise as they shall think fit: And when any of their Places, by Death, Resignation, Deprivation, or otherwise, shall become void, shall and may, within two Months next after such avoidance, by writing under their said Common Seal, nominate and appoint other fit Officers and Soldiers, who have so served in the said Army of Ireland, in the Places of them, and every of them so demising, resigning, or otherwise becoming void; and that in Case the said Governors and their Successors for the time being, or the most Part of them, shall not within two Months after such avoidance, make such Nomination and Appointment as aforesaid, that then, and so often, and so every such Case, it shall and may be lawful, to and for the Lord Lieutenant, Lord Deputy, or other chief Governor or Governors of Our said Realm of Ireland, for the time being, by any Writings under their Hands respectively, to nominate and appoint some such Officers and Soldiers, who have so served in the said Army of Ireland, in, and to the Places void by such Default of the said Governors and their Successors for the time being, or the most Part of them, as aforesaid. And that it shall and may be lawful to and for the said Master, Chaplain, Officers and Soldiers, that shall be from Time to Time placed in the said Hospital, to remain, assemble and cohabit together in the said Hospital. And that the said Governors and their Successors for the time being, or the major part of them, shall and may have full Power and Authority under their Common Seal to make, ordain, set down, and prescribe such Orders, Rules, Statutes and Ordinances, for the Order, Rule and Government of the said Hospital, and every Member thereof, and for, and concerning the naming and electing of such Person and Persons as shall succeed into the Place and Room of any the said Governors, in Case any of the Offices, Commands or Employments, with which the Office of one of the Governors of the said HOSPITAL is hereby appointed to go in Succession, should at any Time hereafter be laid aside, or no longer continued; and for and concerning the Election, Order, Rule, and Government of the Master, Chaplain, and all the Members, Officers, and Servants of the said HOSPITAL, in their several Places, Offices, Rooms, and Employments; and for and concerning their, and every of their Stipends, and Allowances, for and towards their, or any of their Maintenance and Relief, as to the said Governors and their Successors, for the time being, or the major part of them, shall seem most and convenient. And that such Orders, Rules, Statutes and Ordinances, so by them to be set down and prescribed as aforesaid, shall be, stand, and remain in full force, and virtue in Law, and be executed in all Things according to the true intent and meaning thereof, under the several Pains, forfeitures, and Penalties, that shall be expressed and contained in the same Ordinances, Statutes and Rules.

PROVIDED ALWAYS, That the said Rules, Statutes and Ordinances, or any of them, be not repugnant or contrary to the Laws and Statutes of Our said Realm of Ireland, or to any Ecclesiastical Canons or Constitutions of Our Church of Ireland, that shall be then in Force, or Use, nor against the Purport or true Intent of these Our Letters Patents.

And also, that the said Governors and their Successors for the Time being, or the major part of them, shall have full Power and Authority from Time to Time, and as often as they shall think fit and convenient, to visit the said HOSPITAL, and to order, reform and redress all Disorders and Abuses, in and touching the Government thereof, and the Manners of the several Officers, and Members relating thereunto: And further, to Punish, Censure, Suspend, and Deprive the Master, Chaplain, and other Officers and Members of the said HOSPITAL, as to them shall seem just, fit and convenient.

AND FURTHER, of Our like special Grace, certain Knowledge, and mere Motion, by and with Advice and Consent aforesaid, We have Ordained, Declared, and Established, and by these Presents, for Us, Our Heirs and Successors, We do Ordain, Declare, and Establish, that the said Governors and their Successors, shall be, and are hereby wholly and utterly dissolved in Law, to make, do, levy, or suffer any Act or Acts, Thing or Things, whereby or by means whereof, the Site, Circuit, or Precinct of the said HOSPITAL, or the said Sixty four Acres of Land, above mentioned, that are hereby granted by Us to the said Governors and their Successors, for the Use of the said HOSPITAL, or any Part thereof, or any the Houses or Buildings erected, or to be erected thereupon, shall, or may be Aliened, Assured, Given, Granted, Demised, Changed, or in any sort conveyed or come to the Possession of Us, our Heirs, or Successors, or of any other Person or Persons, Bodies Politick or Corporate whatsoever, or to any other Use or Use than what the same are hereby intended for and designed; and that the whole Residue and Remainder of the said Sixty four Acres of Land that is not Inclosed within the Walls and Precinct of the said HOSPITAL now built thereupon, shall be for ever hereafter employed in Building such Out-Houses thereupon, and making such Yards, Gardens, and Walks therein, and to such other Uses as shall be necessary or convenient for the said HOSPITAL, and for the Support, Maintenance and more comfortable Residence of the Members thereof. And that all Alienations, Assurances, Gifts, Grants, Leases, Charges, and Conveyances, whatsoever to be done, suffered, or made, to Us, Our Heirs or Successors, or to any other Person or Persons, Bodies Politick or Corporate whatsoever of the Site, Circuit, or Precinct of the said HOSPITAL, of the said Sixty four Acres of Land herein above mentioned, or any Part thereof, or of any the Houses, or Buildings erected or to be erected thereupon, or of, or out of any part or parcel of them, or any of them, shall be utterly void, and of none Effect, to all Intents, Constructions, and Purposes, any matter or thing to the contrary notwithstanding.

And our Will and Pleasure is, and We do hereby, for Us, Our Heirs and Successors, Ordain, Declare, Constitute and Appoint, That whensoever any of the said Governors herein above mentioned, or any of them, or their or any of their Successors shall die, or be removed from such their Offices, Commands or Employments, whereunto such Place or Places of Governor or Governors of the said HOSPITAL, is hereby annexed, or voluntarily shall relinquish such their Office, and Employments, that then and in such case, the remaining Governors shall still continue and remain Incorporated, as fully and amply, to all Intents and purposes, as the said Governors herein above mentioned are hereby Incorporated; and that in all such Cases, whereto the said Office or Place of Governor is hereby annexed to any Office or Employment, the same shall go in Succession to such as shall next succeed in such Office or Employment; but in Case any of the said Place or Places of Governor or Governors of the said HOSPITAL, shall become void, by means that any of the said Offices or Employments, whereunto the same is hereby annexed, shall be laid aside, or not any longer continued; that then and in such case, the major Part of the Surviving Remaining Governors, shall have full Power and Authority at any Time, within three Weeks after such Place shall so become void, to Name and Elect, Choose and Appoint, some other fit Person or Persons to be the Governor or Governors of the said HOSPITAL, in the Place and Room of each Governor or Governors that shall so become void; and in case no such Election shall be made by the said Governors or the major Part of them, within three Weeks after such Vacancy, it shall and may be lawful, to and for the Lord Lieutenant, Lord Deputy, or other chief Governor or Governors of Our said Realm of Ireland, for the Time being, by Writing under their respective Hands, to nominate any other fit Person or Persons to succeed in the Place or Places of Governor and Governors of the said HOSPITAL, in the Place and Room of such Governor or Governors.

And Our further Will and Pleasure is, and we do hereby Ordain and Appoint, that where the said Office or Place of Governor is hereby appointed, to go in Succession with any the Offices, Commands, and Imployments, wheresoever to the same is hereby annexed, that such Persons shall continue no longer Governors, but only during such Time as they shall continue in their said respective Offices, Commands and Imployments. And that upon their or any of their Removal off of the said Offices, or Commands or Imployments, they shall from thenceforth no longer continue Governors of the said Hospital; and in case any of their said Offices or Commands in the said Army shall be laid aside, or no longer continued, that no Person or Persons shall be Elected or Admitted to succeed in their Place or Places of Governor or Governors of the said Hospital, but such Person or Persons only as at the Time of such Election or Admission shall have been for Ten Years a Commissioned Officer in the said Army of Ireland.

And Our further Will and Pleasure is, and We do hereby for Us, Our Heirs and Successors Ordain, Declare and Appoint, that the Governors of the said Hospital and their Successors, or the major Part of them, shall have, keep, and constantly observe, Four several set Days and Times of their Meeting, for and about the Affairs and Concerns of the said Hospital, either at the said Hospital (if conveniently it may be) or at any other Place by themselves to be appointed for that purpose, on such Days, as by the said Governors of the said Hospital, or the major part of them, or in their Default, by the chief Governor or Governors of Our said Kingdom of Ireland, shall be appointed; and at the said Quarterly Meeting, shall take an Account of the Quarterly Receipts and Payments relating to the said Hospital, and shall and may then also treat on, and dispatch any other Affairs concerning the said Hospital; and shall also hold one other Annual Meeting on such Day, as in like manner shall be (as aforesaid) appointed to take the Year's Account, ending the 25th day of March next preceding such annual Meeting, of the Receipts and Payments relating to the said Hospital, and to view and inform themselves of the Estate thereof; and that the said Governors and their Successors, or the major part of them, may also hold and keep such other occasional Meetings, as upon any emergent Accident shall be found necessary for the Affairs of the said Hospital, Notice being first given to all the Governors that by then residing in or near Our said City of Dublin, of the time and place of such Meeting; and that the said Governors, or the major part of them, then assembled at such occasional Meeting, shall and may Treat, Resolve of, and Determine such Matters relating to the said Hospital, as shall be fit or necessary for their Debate, Judgment, Decision, or Resolution, and that what shall be Resolved and Agreed upon by the major part of the Governors present on such Quarterly, Annual, or Occasional Days of Meeting shall stand good, firm, and effectual, until the same shall be altered, or changed, at some succeeding Meeting of the said Governors, or the major part of them: And that at every, and any such Meeting of the said Governors, each of the Governors then assembled, shall have but one single Vote, notwithstanding that any of them may have two several Offices or Imployments, by reason of such whereof he may, by virtue of these Our Letters Patents, be constituted one of the Governors of the said Hospital: and that the Orders and Resolutions of every such Assembly shall be fairly entered in a Book to be kept for that purpose, by such Register as by the said Governors and their Successors, or the major part of them, shall be appointed to attend them on such Occasions, who is always to be present at such Meetings; and shall also be signed by such of the Governors as shall be present at each Meeting, or the major part of them, within the space of One Month next following the holding of every such Assembly.

And Our further Will and Pleasure is, and We do hereby declare and appoint, that in case any Doubt or Controversy shall happen or arise amongst the said Governors, or their Successors concerning the sense, or meaning of any Clause, Article, or Sentence, in these Our Letters Patents contained, in the Interpretation whereof the said Governors or the major part of them shall not agree, that then, and in such case they may apply themselves to the Lord Lieutenant, Lord Deputy, or other chief Governor or Governors of our said Kingdom of Ireland, whose Resolution or Determination therein being had in Writing, and entered in the Publick Registry of the said Hospital, shall be Final and Conclusive therein: And also that in case any Controversy or Differences shall arise between any the Officers and Members of the said Hospital, that they shall be Heard and Determined by the Master of the said Hospital, or by the Deputy Master during his Sickness or Absence.

And our further Will and Pleasure is, and We do hereby Grant, and Ordain for Us, Our Heirs and Successors, that the Governors of the said Hospital, or the major part of them, shall be, and are hereby Authorized to Administer an Oath to any Person or Persons relating to any the Affairs of the said Hospital; and that their Sentence or Determination therein, being entered in the Publick Registry of the said Hospital, shall be Final and Conclusive to all Parties.

And Our further Will and Pleasure is, and We do hereby Declare, Ordain, and Appoint, that the said Hospital, and the said Sixty four Acres of Land thereunto belonging, and hereby granted by Us for the Use of the said Hospital, and all the Buildings erected or to be erected thereupon, shall for ever hereafter be and continue Freed and Discharged from the Payment of all, and all manner of Rents, Taxes, Subsidies, Chimney-Money, and all other Charges and Payments whatsoever that are, or at any time hereafter shall or may be due or payable to Us, Our Heirs or Successors, or shall or may be Charged or Imposed thereupon, either by Act of Parliament, or otherwise howsoever.

And Our further Will and Pleasure is, and We do hereby, for Us, Our Heirs and Successors, Ordain, Declare, Establish and Appoint, that the aforesaid Deduction of Sixpence in the pound out of the Pay of Our said Army, and other Persons placed upon the Military List of Our Establishment, in Our said Kingdom of Ireland be continued for the Use of the said Hospital, and be also constantly paid to such Person or Persons, as by the Governors of the said HOSPITAL, or the major part of them, shall be from time to time appointed to receive and account for the same.

AND LASTLY, Our Will and Pleasure is, and We do hereby further for Us, Our Heirs and Successors, Ordain and Declare, that the Master Gunner, and other Officers of the Ordnance of Our said Army, in Our said Kingdom of Ireland, shall and may from Time to Time, make such Use of the Gun-Yard, House, and Park, lately erected on Part of the aforesaid Sixty-four Acres of Land, and the Ground staked out, lying East from the said Gun-Yard, containing from three about Two Thousand Six Hundred Feet in Length, and about One Hundred Feet in Breadth, to Exercise the Gunners of Our Train of Artillery that is in such Manner as by the chief Governor or Governors of Our said Kingdom of Ireland, shall be thought fit.

AND FURTHER, Our Will and Pleasure is that these Our Letters Patents, and every Clause, Sentence, and Article therein contained or in the Enrolment thereof, shall be in all and every Thing and Things, firm, good, valid, sufficient and effectual in the Law, unto the said Governors of the said HOSPITAL, and their Successors, according to the Purport and True intent thereof, without any further Grant, Licence, or Toleration, from Us, Our Heirs or Successors to be had, procured, or obtained.

PROVIDED ALWAYS, That these Our Letters Patents be Enrolled in the Rolls of Our High Court of Chancery, in Our said Kingdom of Ireland, within the space of Six Months next ensuing the Date of these Presents; although no express Mention be made of the true yearly Value or Certainty of the Premises, or of any Gifts, or Grants, heretofore made, by Us, or any of Our Progenitors, to these the said Governors of the said HOSPITAL, of the Premises in these Presents; Any Statute, Act, Ordinance, Provision, or Restriction, or any other Cause, Matter, or Thing whatsoever, to the contrary hereof in any wise notwithstanding.

IN WITNESS whereof, We have caused these Our Letters to be made Patents; Witness Our aforesaid Deputy General of Our said Kingdom of Ireland, at Dublin, the Nineteenth Day of February, in the Six and Thirtieth Year of Our Reign.

Irrot' declarac tertio die Martii, Anno Regni Regis Caroli Secundi Tricesimo sexto. Copia Vera

THO. CASTER, D. G. & C. Rot'.

His MAJESTY's Letter for Ground to be Laid to the Hospital.

Signed, CHARLES, R.

"Right Trusty and Right Intirely Beloved Cousin and Counsellor, We greet you well
— Whereas We have directed the Building of an HOSPITAL for the Maintenance and Convenience
— of such aged and maimed Soldiers of Our Army in Ireland, as are or shall be, during their
— Continuance in the said Army, become unserviceable; and the said HOSPITAL is already begun
— to be erected upon part of Our Lands now inclosed in our Park, called the Phœnix Park, near
— the old ruinous Building, commonly called the Castle of Kilmainham. Our Will and Pleasure is,
— That the said Land, whereupon the said HOSPITAL is now building, together with such a
— quantity of Land thereunto adjoining (not exceeding in the whole, Sixty four Acres, Plantation
— tion Measure) as You shall think fit to be laid thereunto, be set apart, and for ever hereafter
— continued for the Use of the said HOSPITAL. And We do hereby authorize you, to cause
— effectual Letters Patents to be passed under the Great Seal of Our said Kingdom of Ireland, to
— such Trustees as You shall nominate, and their Heirs, to the Use of the said HOSPITAL, without
— any rent to be reserved thereon, to Us, Our Heirs, or Successors; to the Intent and Purport
— that when the said HOSPITAL shall be finished and incorporated, the said Lands may be con-
— veyed by the said Trustees to the said Corporation and their Successors for ever. And for so
— doing, these Our Letters shall be your sufficient Warrant, and so We bid You most heartily
— farewell."

Given at Our Court at White-Hall, the 19th Day of April, 1681, in the Three and Thirtieth Year of Our Reign.

By His Majesty's Command,

L. JENKINS.

Entered at the Signet Office the 19th of April, 1681.
Nic. Marius.

To Our Right Trusty and Right
Intirely Beloved Cousin and
Counsellor, James Duke of
Ormond, &c.

(C.)

Orders by the Lord Lieutenant General, and General Governor of Ireland.

"ORMONDE.

"These are to will and require You forthwith, in Pursuance of His Majesty's Letter, under "His Sign Manual, and Privy Signet, unto Us directed, bearing Date the 19th Day of *April*, 1681, "in the Three and Thirtieth Year of His Majesty's Reign, a Copy whereof We herewith send "you, to survey and set out such Quantity of His Majesty's Lands in the *Phœnix* Park, contiguous "to the New HOSPITAL, now in building, for the Relief of aged and maimed Soldiers, as shall not "exceed the Number of Sixty-four Acres Plantation Measure, to be apply'd for the Use of the "said HOSPITAL; and to make a Map, or Draught, of such Lands as you shall so pitch upon for "that Use, and present the same to Us for Our Approbation, that thereupon such further Order "may be given, in pursuance of His Majesty's said Letter, as shall be thought fit; and for so "doing, this shall be your Warrant."

Given at His Majesty's Castle of *Dublin*, the 22d Day of *December*, 1681.

E. GASCOIGN.

To Our Trusty and Well beloved
William Robinson, Esq; Sur-
veyor General.

(D.)

His MAJESTY's Letter for Erecting the Hospital.

Signed, CHARLES, R.

"Right Trusty and Right Intirely Beloved Cousin and Counsellor, We greet you well. "Whereas many of the Soldiers in Our Army in *Ireland*, who are grown Aged, or otherwise "Unserviceable, are yet continued in Our Pay for want of some other fitting Provision for their "Livelihood and Maintenance; and We conceive it unreasonable, that such Persons who have "faithfully served Us in Our Army, whilst their Health and Strength continued, should, when by "Age, Wounds, or other Infirmities, they are disabled from serving Us any longer, be disburdened "without any Care to be taken for their future Subsistence; We thought it necessary for us to "consider of some Way whereby Our Army may be freed from such unserviceable Persons, and "how such of them who shall be dismissed from Our Service, may be afterwards provided for; "and We calling to mind, that upon a Contract made by Us with *Robert* and *William Bridges*, "Gentlemen, for the Advance of the Sum of Thirty Six Thousand, Five Hundred, Sixty Five "Pounds, Four Shillings, and Eleven Pence, Sterling, or thereabouts, to be made by them towards "the discharge of some Arrears of Pay due to Our Army; We were pleased to allow to the said "*Robert* and *William Bridges*, the Sum of Twelve Pence in the Pound, to be deducted out of all "the Pay that should grow due by Our Establishment to Our Military List in Our said Kingdom, "for Eighteen Months, from the 25th day of *September*, in the Year 1677, which did expire on the "25th day of *March* last; We have thought fit that the said Deduction of Twelve Pence in the "Pound be not continued for any longer time, than the same hath been already granted to the "said *Robert* and *William Bridges*; and that from and after the said 25th day of *March* last, there "shall only be deducted Six Pence in the Pound out of all the Pay that afterwards shall grow "due by Our Establishment to Our Military List, and that the same shall be wholly applied "towards making a Provision for such aged and maimed Officers and Soldiers of Our said Army, "as shall not be thought fit to be any longer continued in Our Service. Our Will and Pleasure "therefore is, and We do hereby Authorize and Require You, to cause a Deduction of Six Pence "in the Pound to be from Time to Time made out of all the Pay that from and after the 25th "day of *March* last, shall grow due by the present, or any future Establishment, to any Person "or Persons whatsoever upon Our Military List in Our said Kingdom; and to take care that the "same be paid into the Hands of such Person or Persons as You shall appoint for the Receipt "thereof. And We do hereby give unto You full Power and Authority from Time to Time, to "issue and Employ the same towards the building and settling an HOSPITAL for such aged and "maimed Officers and Soldiers as shall at any Time be dismissed out of Our Army as unservice-"able Men, and for making Provision for their future Maintenance, in such Way and Manner as "you shall think fit: It being Our express Will and Pleasure, That none of the said Money shall "upon any Occasion or Pretence whatsoever be diverted to any other Use, than whereunto the "same is hereby designed. And you are also to take care that such Person or Persons as shall "be so by You appointed to receive the said Money, do first give unto Us good and sufficient "Security for his or their giving a true Account of the said Money, so to be received by him or "them, whensoever he or they shall be thereunto required: And for the Payment thereof, from "Time to Time, according to such Warrants as shall from Time to Time be by You given concern-"ing the same. And also that he or they do at least once every Year, or oftner, as You shall "see cause, give us exact and true Account of such Receipts and Payments, either to You, or "such Persons as You shall appoint to take and audit his said Accounts. And We do hereby "further declare Our Royal Will and Pleasure to be, That no Persons who were either aged, or

" otherwise unserviceable, when they were first taken into Our Army, shall be taken to be such
" prehended within the Provision hereby intended, but only such Persons, who by reason of Age,
" Wounds, or other Infirmities, since their first coming into Our Army, are grown unfit to be
" any longer continued in Our Service. And Our further Pleasure is, That You prepare a
" Draught of such Rules and Orders for the Constitution and Government of the said Hospital
" as You shall think fitting, which You are to transmit unto Us, for Our Royal Consideration and
" Approbation: and for so doing, these Our Letters shall be Your Warrant."

Given at Our Court at *Whitehall*, the 27th day of October, 1679, in the One and Thirtieth
Year of Our Reign.

By His Majesty's Command,

COVENTRY.

To Our Right Trusty and Right
Entirely Well-beloved Cousin
and Counsellor, James Duke of
ORMONDE, Lord Lieutenant-
General of IRELAND, &c.

(E.)

Order by the Lord-Lieutenant and Council.

ORMONDE,

" WHEREAS His Majesty by His Letters dated the 27th of October, 1679, hath directed,
" that from and after the 29th day of March, last, there should be deducted Six Pence in the
" Pound out of all the Pay that afterwards should grow due to the Establishment to the Military
" List, and that the same should be issued and employed towards the building and settling an
" Hospital in this Kingdom, for such aged and maimed Officers and Soldiers, as shall at any
" Time be dismissed the Army, as unserviceable Men; and for making Provision for their future
" Maintenance in such way and manner as We the Lord Lieutenant shall think fit. Now for the
" more equally Execution of his Majesty's said Direction, We think fit, and do accordingly order,
" That *Michael* Lord Arch-Bishop of *Armagh*, Primate and Metropolitan of all *Ireland*, and the
" Lord Arch-Bishop of *Armagh* for the time being, the Lord Chancellor of *Ireland*, and the Lord
" Chancellor or Lord Keeper of the Great Seal for the time being, John Lord Arch-Bishop of
" Dublin, Primate and Metropolitan of *Ireland*, and the Lord Arch-Bishop of Dublin for the time
" being, Richard Earl of *Arran*, Colonel of His Majesty's Regiment of Guards in this Kingdom,
" and the Colonel of the said Regiment for the time being, Richard Earl of *Ranelagh*, His Majesty's
" Vice-Treasurer, and His Majesty's Vice-Treasurer for the time being, *Francis* Earl of *Longford*,
" Master of the Ordnance in Ireland, and the Master of the Ordnance for the time being, *Arthur*
" Lord Viscount *Granard*, Marshal of His Majesty's Army, and the Marshal of the Army for the
" time being, the Lord Viscount *Lanesborough*, *Henry* Lord Bishop of *Meath*, and the Lord Bishop
" of *Meath* for the time being, *Anthony* Lord Bishop of *Kildare*, and the Lord Bishop of *Kildare* for
" the time being, Sir Charles *Meredith*, Knight, Chancellor of His Majesty's Court of Exchequer,
" and the Chancellor of the Exchequer for the time being, Sir Robert *Booth*, Knight, Lord Chief
" Justice of the King's Bench, and the Lord Chief Justice of the King's Bench for the time being,
" John *Keating*, Esquire, Lord Chief Justice of His Majesty's Court of Common Pleas, and the
" Lord Chief Justice of the said Court for the time being, the Lord Chief Baron of His Majesty's
" Court of Exchequer for the time being, Sir John Davis, Knight, His Majesty's Principal Secretary
" of State in *Ireland*, and the Secretary of State for the time being, Sir William *Flower*, Knight,
" Lieutenant Colonel of His Majesty's Regiment of Guards, and the Lieutenant Colonel of the
" said Regiment for the time being, Anthony *Hungerford*, Esquire, Captain of His Majesty's Guards
" of Horse, and the Captain of the said Guards for the time being, Sir William Davis, Knight, His
" Majesty's Prime Serjeant at Law, and His Majesty's Prime Serjeant for the time being,
" Sir William *Domvile*, Knight, His Majesty's Attorney General, and the Attorney General for the
" time being, and Sir John *Temple*, Knight, His Majesty's Solicitor General, and the Solicitor
" General for the time being, or any Three or more of them, be, and are hereby appointed a
" Standing Committee, who are to treat for Artists, Workmen, and other Persons, and after
" receiving Proposals from them, to treat and agree with them for providing and buying
" Materials for the erecting, building, and finishing of the said intended Hospital, in such manner
" as they the said Committee shall think fit, and to nominate and appoint such Officers and
" Overseers in the Service, as shall be found necessary: and also some fit Person as Treasurer, to
" receive and issue the Money, designed for the Use of the said Hospital, and to settle such
" Allowances for the said Treasurer, Officers, and Overseers, as shall be fit; And they are also to
" do all such other Acts and Things as they shall conceive requisite and necessary for the carrying
" on of the said Work; and from Time to Time to prepare Warrants to be signed by Us the Lord
" Lieutenant, for the issuing of the said Money, in such proportions and manner as they shall
" think fit. And the said Committee are to prepare a Draught of Rules, Orders, and Directions
" for the Constitution and Government of the said Hospital, and present the said Draught to Us
" the Lord Lieutenant, to be transmitted to His Majesty, for His Royal Consideration and Appro-
" bation: And they are to meet on Tuesday next, and once a Week after, and oftner as there shall

" be Occasion, and to adjourn from Time to Time, and from Place to Place, as they shall see
" cause; and to return to Us the Lord Lieutenant from Time to Time, an Account of their
" Proceedings herein."

Given at the Council Chamber in Dublin, the 27th Day of February, 1679.

Mich. Armach. C. Jo. Dublin, Arran, Langford. Loughborough, Gr. Dillon, Cha. Meredith,
Robert Booths, John Keating, John Davis.

(F.)

An Account of Money expended in building the ROYAL HOSPITAL of King CHARLES the
Second, from March 8, 1680, to December 25, 1686, &c.

Paid to several Workmen and Others, for Work and Materials, for building the said HOSPITAL, as
follows, viz.

	£	s.	d.
To Labourers for digging Foundations, Cellars, &c.	508	12	00
To Day-Labourers,	557	17	10
To Masons and Brick-layers,	5425	07	04
To Stone-Cutters,	1248	21	07
To Carpenters,	1450	03	04
To Sawyers,	977	17	11
To Joyners and Carvers,	990	13	01
To Plasterers and Painters,	1935	07	01
To Smiths and Iron Mongers,	1022	19	02
To Plumbers,	1081	04	10
To Slaters,	801	15	06
To Glaziers,	319	12	00
To Turners,	6	10	00
To Pavers,	15	13	07
To Tile-Makers for Tiles,	156	14	07
For Timber, Deal, and Laths,	5541	00	00
For Portland Stones, and other Hewing Stones,	1160	16	00
For Carriage and Freight of Timber, Stone, Lead, &c.	971	17	02
For Tools, Instruments, and other Contingencies,	120	16	03
To Overseers, and other Officers for their Salaries,	810	00	00
For an Engine to raise Water for the Work-House,	37	10	00
Total expended in building the Hospital, Infirmary, Gardens, Church-Yard-Walls, &c.	22459	10	11½

(G.)

The Charter Granted by His Majesty George II.

GEORGE THE SECOND by the Grace of God, of Great Britain, France, and Ireland, King,
Defender of the Faith, and so forth. TO ALL unto whom these Presents shall come, Greeting.
WHEREAS Our Royal Predecessor King Charles the Second, by His Letters Patents, bearing Date
the Nineteenth Day of February, in the Thirty-sixth Year of His Reign, did Erect and Endow an
HOSPITAL near Dublin, for the Relief and Support of antient and maimed Officers and Soldiers of the
Army of Ireland; and did thereby grant, declare, ordain, constitute and appoint the Lord Lieutenant,
Lord Deputy, or other chief Governor or Governors of Our said Kingdom of Ireland, for the time
being, and the several other Officers, in the said Letters Patents, particularly mentioned, and their
Successors for ever, to be Governors of the said HOSPITAL, and of the Members, Goods, Lands,
Revenues, and Hereditaments of the same; and that the same Governors and their Successors for
ever should be a Body Politick and Corporate, to have a Continuance for ever by the Name of, THE
GOVERNORS OF THE HOSPITAL OF KING CHARLES THE SECOND, for maimed and
antient Officers and Soldiers of the Army of Ireland, and did thereby grant to the said Governors and
their Successors, several Lands, Tenements, Hereditaments, Estates, Rights, Titles, Powers, Authorities, Privileges, and Franchises, necessary and convenient for the due Regulation and Government, as
well as for the Support and Continuance of the said HOSPITAL for ever; and appointed quarterly and
annual Meetings, and other occasional Meetings when necessary, to be held by the said Governors or
the major part of them, for the Affairs of the said HOSPITAL, as by the said Letters Patents, Relation
being thereunto had, may more fully and at large appear.

AND WHEREAS it has been represented unto Us, that many of the Governors of the said
HOSPITAL being of high Rank in Our Army, who from their Stations therein, are often obliged to
be Resident in Our Kingdom of Great Britain, and others of the said Governors to be absent from
Dublin upon Our necessary Service; a major part of the Governors of this said HOSPITAL can seldom
be brought together to transact the Business of the said HOSPITAL, to the great Detriment thereof.

E 2

AND WHEREAS it would more effectually Answer all the Ends proposed by the said Letters Patent, if any Seven or more of the said Governors, instead of the major part of them, were Impowered to Exercise all the said Powers and Authorities granted to the Governors of the said Hospital, by the said Letters Patent.

KNOW YE therefore that We of Our more special Grace, certain Knowledge and mere Motion, by and with the Advice and Consent of Our Right Trusty and Right Intirely Beloved Cousin and Counsellor, John Duke of Bedford, Our Lieutenant General and General Governor of Our said Kingdom of Ireland, and according to the Tenor and Effect of Our Letters, under Our Privy Signet and Sign Manual, bearing Date at Our Court at St. James's the Twenty-ninth Day of March, One Thousand Seven Hundred and Fifty-eight, in the Thirty-first Year of Our Reign, and now Enrolled in the Rolls of Our High Court of Chancery in Our said Kingdom of Ireland, have confirmed, and by these Presents for Us, Our Heirs and Successors, We do Confirm to the said Governors of the said Hospital and their Successors, all Lands, Tenements, Hereditaments, Estates, Rights, Titles, Interests, Powers, and Authorities, granted to them by the said Letters Patents of Our Royal Predecessor King Charles the Second.

AND FURTHER of Our like special Grace, certain Knowledge and mere Motion, by and with the Advice and Consent aforesaid, WE DO hereby for Us, Our Heirs and Successors, grant to the said Governors of the said Hospital, and their Successors, that they the said Governors and their Successors, or any Seven or more of them, shall and may from Time to Time, and at all Times hereafter, assemble and meet together at such Times, and in such like Manner, as the said Governors, by the said Letters Patent, are directed and appointed to meet, for and about the Affairs and Concerns of the said Hospital, and being so met together, shall and may Use and Exercise all and every the Powers and Authorities granted to the said Governors by the said Letters Patent, for the Government and Regulation of the said Hospital, in as full and ample Manner as the said Governors, or the major part of them, may now Use or Exercise the same; (except only the Appointment of a Master of the said Hospital) who Our Will and Pleasure is, shall from Time to Time, and at all Times hereafter, be chosen and constituted by the said Governors, or the major part of them, by Instrument under their Hands and Common Seal, in such Manner, as by the said Letters Patent is directed and appointed, and not otherwise.

PROVIDED ALWAYS, That these Our Letters Patent be enrolled in the Rolls of Our High Court of Chancery, in Our said Kingdom of Ireland, within the space of Six Months next ensuing the Date of these Presents.

IN WITNESS whereof, We have caused these Our Letters to be made Patent; Witness Our aforesaid Lieutenant General and General Governor of Our said Kingdom of Ireland, at Dublin, the Twenty-fourth Day of April, in the Thirty-first Year of Our Reign.

Dunnill.

Erd. Michael Newland, D. Clerk of the Crown and Hanaper.

(Seal)

Enrolled in the Office of the Rolls of His Majesty's High Court of Chancery in Ireland, the 9th Day of May, in the 31st Year of the Reign of King George the Second, and examined by

John Lodge, Deputy Clerk and Keeper of the Rolls.

(H.)

ROYAL WARRANT OF 16th DECEMBER, 1843.

VICTORIA R.

Our will and pleasure is, that the following shall be the Establishment, Duties, Salaries, and Allowances in Money and in Kind, for the Officers, Under Officers, and Servants belonging to Our Royal Hospital at Kilmainham, in Our County of Dublin, viz:—

Establishments and Duties	Salaries and Allowances in Money per Annum	Allowances in Kind	
Master — To exercise a general superintendence and control over the whole of the establishment.	Salary, —. Allowance for garden, 11l.	Apartments furnished; coals-houses and stabling necessary to the number of horses for which he is allowed forage; 30 tons of coals, 500 lbs. of candles.	To be held by the General Officer Commanding the troops for the time being.
Deputy Master — To execute under the Master, or in his absence, a general superintendence and control over the whole establishment.	Salary, —.	Apartments furnished; coals-houses and stabling according to the number of horses for which the officer's salary gives an allowance of forage; 20 tons coals, [illegible] lbs. candles.	To be held jointly by the Surgeon-Adjutant-General and Deputy Quartermaster-General in Dublin, each having a salary of [illegible] per annum. [illegible] coals, and 100 lbs. candles.
Assistant — To attend the invalids at all parades, chapel assemblies, dinner, [illegible], &c., and to investigate cases of absence therefrom.	Salary, 150l. 10s.	Apartments unfurnished; stabling, or an allowance of 10l. a year to provide it. Coals to be always warm on duty. 6 tons coals, 100 lbs. candles.	To be a substitute from the half-pay list, but not to draw his half-pay. May receive pension for wounds, if entitled.
First Invalid Captains — To attend on the invalids at their respective companies, and to turn in parties, the daily duty of Orderly Captain. To attend with the Quartermaster or Steward in the kitchen to inspect provisions furnished by the contractors. To see that the rooms and galleries of the hospital are properly cleaned. In the absence of the Master and Deputy Master the Senior Captain to undertake the procurement of the Hospital.	Salary of the four established at 97l. 10s.	Apartments unfurnished; coals; stabling, or an allowance of 10l. a year each to provide it. Coals to be always warm on duty. 3 tons of coals, 140 lbs. candles, each.	Two to be Captains, with their half-pay ready to be his did a day. Two to be Lieutenants, with their half-pay made up to be a day. May receive pension for wounds, if entitled.
Secretary and Treasurer — To attend the meetings of the Governors and record their proceedings; to prepare and submit to them all matters requiring their consideration; to conduct the correspondence of the establishment; to pay all expenses and keep the accounts.	Salary, —. (Sinecure.)	Apartments unfurnished; 3 tons of coals, 140 lbs. of candles.	The present holder to have the sinecure salary, in continuation of his long service; his successor to have less, increasing by 10l. every two years to hold.
Clerk to Secretary and Treasurer — To copy all correspondence, and perform all the writing of the Secretary's office.	Salary, 100l. (Sinecure.)	Apartments unfurnished; 3 tons coals, 50 lbs. candles.	Salary to increase from 50l. to 100l. by 10l. every two years. The present holder to have this scale of salary.
Chaplain — To read prayers twice every day in the Hospital, and twice every week in the infirmary; to preach on Sundays; to visit the sick, and to bury the dead.	Salary, 100l.	Apartments unfurnished; 3 tons coals, 100 lbs. candles.	

Establishment and Duties	Salaries and Allowances in Money per Annum	Allowances in Kind	
Physician and Surgeon	Salary, £...	Apartments unfurnished; 4 tons coals, 110 lbs candles.	To be a Surgeon from the half-pay list, but not to draw his half-pay.
Quartermaster, or Steward	Salary, £...	Apartments unfurnished; 4 tons of coal, 110 lbs candles, and sheeting as the Adjutant.	To be a Subaltern or Quartermaster from the half-pay list, but not to draw his half-pay.
Quartermaster-Serjeant	Salary, £...	Two rooms unfurnished; 1 ton of coal, 55 lbs candles. To be clothed and victualled as a Serjeant of In-Pensioners.	To be a Serjeant from the out-pension list, but not to draw his pay.
Matron and Washer	Salary, £...	Apartments unfurnished; 4 tons of coals, 55 lbs of candles.	To be a widow of an officer of the army.
To the Governor	£...		
	£...		

It is Our further will and pleasure, that the appointment of the officers to execute jointly the office of Deputy Master, and the appointment of the Secretary, do commence from the date of this Our Warrant, and that the Establishment of the other officers, under officers, and servants, do commence and take place from time to time only as vacancies may occur in any of the existing situations or appointments, or when a saving corresponding to the amount of any addition shall have been previously effected by death or otherwise in Our said Royal Hospital, according to the discretion of Our Governor or Commissioners for managing the affairs thereof; and these are to annul and make void all grants of offices, salaries, or allowances in money or in kind whatsoever not contained in this Establishment, when the same shall be carried into full effect, and to direct that no new charge be added thereunto without being first sanctioned by Our High Treasurer or the Commissioners of Our Treasury for the time being, upon the recommendation of Our Secretary at War.

Given at Our Court at Windsor Castle, this sixteenth day of December, 1845, in the Ninth year of Our reign.

By Her Majesty's Command,

(Signed)   HENRY GOULBURN.
               HENRY BARING.
               WILLIAM CRIPPS.

(I.)

ROYAL WARRANT OF 15TH JANUARY, 1854.

VICTORIA R.

Our will and pleasure is, that the following shall be the Establishment, Duties, Salaries, and Allowances in Money and in Kind, for the Officers, Under Officers, Soldiers, and Servants, belonging to Our Royal Hospital at Kilmainham, in Our County of Dublin, viz.:—

Establishment and Duties.	Salaries and Allowances in Money per Annum.	Allowances in Kind.	Qualifications and Remarks.
MASTER ... ... To execute a general superintendence and control over the whole establishment.	Salary, &c. Allowances for his garden, &c.	Furnished apartments, coals, candles, and stabling, according to the number of horses for which he is allowed forage, or Gun, in order of his Forage, [illegible] tons of coal, [illegible] the candles.	Appointment to be held by the General officer commanding the troops for the time being, who shall not retain salary or other military allowances, except as stated.
DEPUTY MASTER ... ... To execute under the Master, or in his absence, a general superintendence and control over the whole establishment.	Salary, &c. ...	Furnished apartments, coals, and stabling, according to the number of horses for which forage allowances are entitled, or forage in money only; [illegible] of coals, and [illegible] lbs. of candles between them.	Appointment to be held jointly by the Deputy Adjutant-General and the Deputy Quartermaster-General for Ireland, but without salary or other military allowances.
TWO CAPTAINS OF INVALIDS ... ... To attend to the discipline of their respective companies, and so forth to perform the daily duty of Orderly Captain. The Captain on duty to attend with the Quartermaster and Steward in the kitchen at breakfast provisions furnished by the contractor; to see that the rooms and galleries of the hospital are properly cleaned, and to be present at the performance of the [illegible] officers and men. In the absence of the Master and Deputy Master, the senior Captain to undertake the government of the Hospital.	Salary, £172. 14s.	Unfurnished apartments, lighting (but without candles), or an allowance in lieu thereof of 44l. per annum each; 4 tons of coal, and 100 lbs. of candles each.	To be Captains, with their half-pay made up to 7s. 6d. a day each.
SECRETARY AND TREASURER ... ... To attend the meetings of the Governors and record their proceedings. To prepare and submit to them all papers requiring their consideration. To conduct the correspondence of the establishment; to pay all expenses, and keep the accounts.	£[illegible] ...	Unfurnished apartments; 4 tons of coal, and 100 lbs. of candles.	To have title on first appointment, increasing by £[illegible] every two years to hold.
CHAPLAIN ... ... To read prayers twice every day in the Hospital, and twice every week in the Infirmary; to preach on Sundays; to visit the sick, and bury the dead.	£[illegible] ...	Unfurnished apartments; 4 tons of coal, and 100 lbs. of candles.	
Roman Catholic clergyman officiating to the pensioners.	£[illegible]		
PHYSICIAN AND SURGEON ... ... To perform the whole medical duty of the establishment; to bestow a constant care upon the sick and wounded soldiers in the Hospital, and attend a proper diet for them.	£[illegible] ...	Unfurnished apartments; 4 tons of coal, and 100 lbs. of candles.	To be a military medical officer, if appointed from the Half-pay List, to draw his half-pay, but only so much besides of his salary as together will make up £[illegible] per annum.
APOTHECARY ... ... To compound all quantities of the [illegible] [illegible] [illegible] Surgery, having day, and to discharge under the Quartermaster and Steward daily with a return of the number of men to be placed on the house diet, and given to the Infirmary, &c. so forthright, and of the items that; to enter the same in a book to be kept [illegible]	£[illegible] ...	Unfurnished apartments; 4 tons of coal, and 100 lbs. of candles.	To be a subaltern officer from the Half-pay List, which allowances he may receive in addition to his pay as Apothecary.

Establishment and Duties.	Salaries and Allowances in Money per Annum.	Allowances in Kind.	Qualifications and Remarks.
Steward—continued.			
for that purpose; to sign an abstract thereof, which the Quartermaster and Steward will prepare, and furnish monthly to the Treasurer, with a view to enable that officer to check the contractor's accounts of provisions issued for the use of the pensioners, and pay for the same, if correct; to prepare a return or return, as may be required, and furnish the Treasurer with a nominal roll of the men in the house, on or before the 1st of each month, in order to enable the Treasurer to issue to those their respective authorized rates of pay, &c.			
QUARTERMASTER AND STEWARD	£65 ..	Unfurnished apartments; 6 tons of coal, and 100 lbs. of candles.	To be a subaltern officer from the Half-pay List, which allowance he may receive in addition to his pay as Quartermaster and Steward.
To attend in the pensioners' kitchen and hall every morning; to see that the provisions of every description are good and wholesome, and fit in every respect for the use, and that they are properly cooked and served out in due form, at the hours prescribed for that purpose; to take charge of the clothing, furniture, and appliances of every description, and superintend the receipt and issue thereof, in accordance with the instructions from the Governor, and the established usages of the house; to prepare and furnish the Treasurer with all necessary receipts, to enable him to check the supplies made by the contractors and others, and to pay for the same when due; to superintend all in-pensioners employed in the cooking or other duties authorized by the warrant, and connected with the establishment; and furnish the Treasurer weekly or monthly, as may be required, with a nominal roll thereof, to enable that officer to pay them their respective allowances.			
CLERK IN SECRETARY AND TREASURER ..	£50 ..	Unfurnished apartments; 6 tons of coal, and 60 lbs. of candles.	To have full, on first appointment, increasing by £5L every two years to £65L.
To copy all correspondence, and perform all the duties of the Secretary and Treasurer's office.			
MATRON AND WASHER	£L ..	Unfurnished apartments; 6 tons of coal, and 70 lbs. of candles.	To be selected for fitness and efficiency, being the widow of an officer in the army; may receive her pension as such, if she have any.
To superintend the nurses, and see that they perform their duties, and do the washing in the Hospital.			
QUARTERMASTER-SERGEANT AND CLERK TO THE QUARTERMASTER AND STEWARD	£d. £d.	Two rooms unfurnished; 1 ton of coals, and 40 lbs. candles. To be clothed and victualled as a corporal of the band.	To be selected, as far as practicable, with regard to twelve fitness, from among such pensioners as were discharged from the army with the rank of sergeant; but with the approbation of the Secretary at War, he may be appointed from any corps if fit to so duty; otherwise. If under the duty 10 years' service to have, on the recommendation of the Secretary at War to the Commissioners of Chelsea Hospital, an addition to his pay-pension and travelling 1d. a day.
To attend under the directions of the Quartermaster every morning in the kitchen, to receive provisions and to see all issued; to divide and distribute the issues; to write out all returns and accounts, and to perform such other duties as may be required by the Quartermaster in the due execution of his duty.			
NURSE TENDERS, &c. ..	..	A room, with allowance of coals and candles, and a gown and pattens of good cheap cotton for ordinary.	To be appointed with reference to their value fitness by the duties they will have to perform. The orders of medical men apply; these widows whose husbands were killed in battle, or died while on foreign service, receiving pension, to have a preference.
Two at 1s. 6d. each per diem, board wages ..	£ s. d. 54 15 0		
One at 1s. 3d. each per diem, board wages ..	45 12 0		
Four at 1s. each per diem, board wages ..	73 0 0		
	173 7s. 0d.		
To take care of such men as are not able to leave their rooms, and clean and regulate their rooms, and to give a constant attendance upon the sick soldiers in the infirmary.			

Establishment and Duties.	Salaries and Allowances in Money per Annum.	Allowances in Kind.	Qualifications and Remarks.
For Companies of In-Pensioners, not to exceed in the whole 210 men, viz. — £ s. d.	.. ..	To be victualled, lodged, and clothed, according to the established rules of the house.	*(text illegible)*
1 Sergeant-Major, at 2s. 6d. a day			
4 Company Sergeants, at 1d. a day	72 18 0		
4 Corporals, at 6d. a day	36 10 0		
3 Drummers, at 6d. a day	18 5 0		
16 Privates, 1st Class, at 8d. a day	29 6 0		
12 Privates, 2nd Class, at 1s. d. a day	18 12 0		
12 Privates, 2nd Class, at 1d. a day	111 0 0		
	£204. 17s. 14. ..		
To the Commissioners or Governors, to cover the expense of employing In-Pensioners in the performance of the under-mentioned duties, each of twenty-six shillings annually for the whole number, viz. —	2884	As all these appointments will be held by In-Pensioners, they will of course receive their pay, rations, clothing, &c., as such In-Pensioners.	*(text illegible)*
At Chapel Clerk, Waterman and Attendant, Ledger Keeper, Infirmary Sergeants, Porter to Dispensary, Cook and Assistant, Messenger to Secretaries, Hall Keeper, Barbers, Coal Porter, Sergeant, &c., Porter to Burial Ground.			
	2,884. 14s. 7d.		

It is Our further will and pleasure, that the Establishment of officers and servants for Our Royal Hospital at Kilmainham do commence from and take place from time to time, only as vacancies shall occur in any of the existing situations or appointments, by death or otherwise, in Our said Royal Hospital, but the vacancies among the soldiers or in-pensioners shall not be filled up after the 31st March next, according to the discretion of Our Governors or Commissioners for managing the affairs thereof; and, except as before excepted, these are to annul and make void all grants of office, salaries, or allowances in money or in kind whatsoever, not contained in this Establishment, when the same shall be carried into full effect, and to direct that no new charge shall be added thereunto without being first sanctioned by Our High Treasurer, or Commissioners of Our Treasury for the time being, upon the recommendation of Our Secretary at War.

Given at Our Court at St. James's, this Twelfth day of January, 1854, in the Seventeenth year of Our reign.

By Her Majesty's Command.

(Signed) ELCHO.
ALFRED HERVEY.

(A true Copy.)
CHARLES W. PENGELLEY, Secretary.

(J.)

RETURN showing the ages of Out-Pensioners admitted to the In-pension List of the Royal
Hospital at Kilmainham from the 1st January, 1857, to 1st October, 1870.

Age on Admission.	Number Admitted.
From 25 to 29	4
30 „ 34	14
35 „ 39	29
40 „ 44	42
45 „ 49	34
50 „ 54	29
55 „ 59	38
60 „ 64	51
65 „ 69	80
70 „ 74	17
75 „ 79	7
80 „ 84	1
85	3
86	3
87	0
88	1
89	1
	451

Average age on admission 56

G. F. DUKE, Secretary and Treasurer.

(K.)

IN-PENSION RETURN, Royal Hospital, Kilmainham, from 1st January, 1856, to 1st October, 1870.

Year.	Number of Applications for Admission to the In-Pension.	Number Admitted to the In-Pension.	Number of Applications for Re-Admission.	Number Re-Admitted after having left.
1856	not recorded	21	not recorded	8
1857	54	23	3	7
1858	57	24	2	2
1859	34	14	2	1
1860	50	26	2	3
1861	38	12	4	2
1862	47	20	4	1
1863	34	17	2	3
1864	57	30	3	8
1865	36	18	1	0
1866	68	19	6	3
1867	67	20	3	3
1868	37	21	2	3
1869	44	14	2	1
1870 (9 months)	35	20	1	1
Totals ..	555	222	43	52

Average Annual Number of Admissions and Re-Admissions, 54.

NOTE.—Of the admissions in this Return five were made to vacancies which existed in December 1856.

G. F. DUKE, Secretary and Treasurer.

L.

RETURN showing the number of In-Pensioners of the Royal Hospital at Kilmainham who have died from 1st January, 1856, to 1st October, 1870, showing the Ages at which they Died.

Deaths in each Year.		Age at Death.		Number of Deaths.
Year.	Number of Deaths.			
1856	11	From 29 to 34 inclusive	4	
1857	12	„ 35 „ 39 „	10	
1858	15	„ 40 „ 44 „	15	
1859	11	„ 45 „ 49 „	12	
1860	16	„ 50 „ 54 „	13	
1861	20	„ 55 „ 59 „	21	
1862	30	„ 60 „ 64 „	17	
1863	14	„ 65 „ 69 „	26	
1864	14	„ 70 „ 74 „	44	
1865	11	„ 75 „ 79 „	34	
1866	10	„ 80 „ 84 „	22	
1867	15	„ 85 „ 89 „	9	
1868	16	91	1	
1869	14	92	1	
1870 (9 months)	12	93	1	
Total	234		234	

Of the above number, one committed suicide.

Average number of deaths per annum ... 16 2/14
Average age at death ... ... 65 9/14 years.

G. F. DUXE, Secretary and Treasurer.

(M.)

RETURN showing the number of Men discharged from the Royal Hospital, Kilmainham, from 1st January, 1856, to 1st October, 1870.

Year.	Removed at their own request.	Dismissed.	Sent to Lunatic Asylum.
1856	11	4	
1857	6	3	
1858	10	8	
1859	5	8	1
1860	5	8	1
1861	5	3	
1862	4	9	
1863	4	6	
1864	4	8	1
1865	5	5	1
1866	5	5	1
1867	11	4	
1868	5	4	
1869 (9 months)	5	5	
Totals	95	85	6

Average annually returned at their own request ... 6 6/14
Average annually dismissed 5 15/14
Average annually sent to Lunatic Asylum ... 6/14
Total 6 6/14

G. F. DUXE, Secretary and Treasurer.

(N.)

FORM sent to the Staff Officer of Pensioners in the case of a man who applies from the Dublin District.

Pension.	Name.	Regiment.

Character on discharge? _____
Present character? _____
Number of family? _____
Remarks _____

Referred to the Staff Officer of Pensioners, Dublin District, for report.

ROYAL HOSPITAL, KILMAINHAM.

Date _____

Secretary.

(D.)

FORM sent to the Staff Officer of Pensioners in the case of a man who applies from a Country District.

INFORMATION necessary to be furnished by an Out-Pensioner of Chelsea Hospital, who wishes to become a Candidate for admission on the In-Pension of the Royal Hospital, Kilmainham.

State your Christian and Surname, and the Regiment from which you were admitted a Pensioner, the period of your service, the rate of your Pension, the date of your admission on the Pension List, and your rank on leaving the service	
Mention any other Regiments in which you have served	
State your present age, and the cause of discharge, if from disability, whether same is the effect of climate or service	
Have you ever served abroad? if so, state where, and the period of such service ..	
If you have served in any action, state the name of it	
If you have been wounded, state in what part of your body, and in what action you received the said wound	
If you have a family, state the number of which the same consists, and how they will be provided for in the event of your being admitted an In-Pensioner	
What is your precise address, and in what Staff District do you receive your Out-Pension?	
Do you belong to the Local Company? ..	
Character on discharge	

_____ certify that _____ is not labouring under any degree of mental derangement, nor infected with any contagious disorder, and that he is unable to labour for a living.

_____ Surgeon.

The character of _____ has been _____
and he has been paid his pension up to _____

Staff Officer of Pensioners,
District.

Dated _____

(P.)

STATEMENT of the Present Staff of Officers, Under Officers, and In-Pensioners of the Royal Hospital, Kilmainham.

[For Dublin, see Royal Warrant of 18th January, 1854 (Appendix, page 61).]

No.	Rank.	Pay.	Allowances.	Remarks.
1	Master	Nil.	Furnished apartments, stabling, coals and candles, 105l. per annum for quarters.	The Lieutenant-General Commanding the Forces.
1	Joint Deputy Master	Nil.	Furnished house, stabling, coals, and candles.	The Deputy Adjutant-General.
1	Joint Deputy Master	Nil.	Nil.	The Deputy Quartermaster-General.
1	Chaplain	250l. a year	Unfurnished apartments, coals, and candles.	
1	Secretary and Treasurer		Ditto	
1	Physician and Surgeon		Ditto	
1	Captain of Invalids	127l. 14s.	Ditto, and 18l. a-year each in lieu of clothing.	
1	Adjutant	7s.	Unfurnished apartments, coals, and candles.	
1	Quartermaster		Ditto	
1	Clerk to Secretary		Ditto	
1	Matron		Ditto	
1	Roman Catholic Clergyman		Nil.	Non-resident.
1	Quartermaster-Sergeant	1s. a-day	Apartments partly furnished, coals and candles, clothing as a staff-sergeant, rations as an in-pensioner.	An in-pensioner.
3	Porters		In rooms each, unfurnished, coals, candles, and green and garden manure	The widows of soldiers.
1	In charge of gardens	1s. a-day	An in-pensioner	This duty is now performed by an in-pensioner instead of a groom.
1	Sergeant-Major			
4	Corporals			
6	Corporals		In-pensioners attended, lodged and clothed, according to the established rules of the house.	
3	Drummer			
10	Privates, 1st class			
20	2nd			

CHARGES upon the sum of 960l. granted to the Governors of Kilmainham Hospital to cover the expenses of employing In-Pensioners in the performance of the following duties.

No.	Rank.	Pay.	Per Annum.	Remarks.
1	Infirmary Sergeant	1s. 6d. a-day	£ s. d. 43 15 0	Granted as extra 1s. a-day by War Office authority, and permitted to retain his own pension.
			Apartment partly furnished, coals and candles, clothing as a staff-sergeant, and rations as an in-pensioner.	
2	Cooks		40 16 0	In-pensioners.
2	Assistant Cooks		37 7 0	An in-pensioner.
1	Waterman		18 7 0	
1	Bell Keeper		18 4 0	
1	Chapel Clerk		18 4 0	
1	Orderly of Infirmary		18 4 0	
1	Messenger, Boardroom		18 13 0	
5	Porters		43 10 0	In-pensioners.
3	Barbers		11 5 0	An in-pensioner.
1	In charge of gas-mains		7 6 0	An in-pensioner.
1	Burial Ground		8 8 0	
1	Arms, Great Hall		8 8 0	
1	Lodge Keeper		9 8 0	
			399 17 0	
	Amount expended		946 17 0	
	Defect, specially authorised by War Office		14 10 0	
			960 7 0	

G. F. DUNN,
Secretary and Treasurer.

N.B.—The Quartermaster-Sergeant and Infirmary Sergeant are included in the Establishment of 192l, but the latter is included in the list of charges on the way of pills.

(Q.)

RETURN showing the numbers refused Admission to the Royal Hospital at Kilmainham from 1st January, 1857, to 1st October, 1870.

Year.	No.	Remarks.
1857	13	Some were rejected as being able to support themselves ; some for bad and indifferent characters ; some as lunatics ; and a few as belonging to the East India Company Service ; others on account of their service being short and disability unestablished.
1858	9	
1859	4	
1860	7	
1861	5	
1862	14	
1863	7	
1864	3	
1865	3	
1866	4	
1867	1	
1868	4	
1869	7	
1870	8	
	89	

G. F. DUNN,
Secretary and Treasurer.

(R.)

RETURN showing the Rates of Out-Pension of Men admitted to the In-Pension List of the Royal Hospital, Kilmainham, from 1st January, 1857, to 1st October, 1870.

Rate of Out-Pension.	Number of Men Admitted and Re-admitted.	Rate of Out-Pension.	Number of Men Admitted and Re-admitted.
s. d.		*s. d.*	Brought forward
At 0 6 a day	5	At 1 0½ a day	200
" 0 6½ "	7	" 1 1 "	6
" 0 6 "	8	" 1 1½ "	4
" 0 7 "	76	" 1 2 "	2
" 0 7 "	26	" 1 2½ "	2
" 0 8 "	10	" 1 3 "	2
" 0 8½ "	46	" 1 4 "	1
" 0 9 "	1	" 1 4½ "	1
" 0 9½ "	17	" 1 5 "	1
" 0 10 "	3	" 1 6½ "	1
" 0 10½ "	60	" 1 8 "	1
" 0 11 "	70	" 1 9 "	1
Carried forward	680	Total	391

G. F. DUNN,
Secretary and Treasurer.

(S.)

ROYAL HOSPITAL, KILMAINHAM.

RETURN of the number of In-Pensioners who are Married.

28th October, 1872.

Number whose Wives live near the Hospital.	Number whose Wives live in the Country.	Total.	Number having Families.	Number having no Family.	Total.
20	6	26	3 6 children	22	24

NUMBER of Married In-Pensioners (whose Wives live near the Hospital) who are Employed, and rates of Pay per annum.

Number	Distribution.	Rate per Annum.
		£ s. d.
1	Waterman	18 4 0
1	Hall Keeper	18 4 0
1	In charge of Galleries	18 4 0
1	Orderly at Infirmary	18 4 0
2	House Porters, each	14 14 0
1	Barber	9 2 6
1	In charge of gas meters	9 2 6
1	Lodge Keeper	9 2 6
9		

WM. McGILL, Captain,
Adjutant, Royal Hospital.

(T.)

RETURN showing the number of Rooms occupied by others than the In-pensioners and Staff belonging to the Royal Hospital, Kilmainham.

		No.	Room	
1		"	2	"
2		"	3	"
3		"	4	" The Assistant Military Secretary's Quarters.
4		"	5	"
5		"	6	"
6		"	7	" Assistant Military Secretary's Office.
7		"	8	"
8		"	9	"
9		"		" Aide-de-Camp's Quarters.
10	Ground Floor ..	"	10	"
11		"	11	" Office and Stores of Out-Pensioners.
12		"	12	"
13		"	13	"
14		"	14	"
15		"	15	" Aide-de-Camp's Waiting Room.
16		"	17	"
17		"	23	" General's Private Office.
18		"	20	" Aide-de-Camp's Quarters.
19	Middle Gallery ..	"	22	"
20	Upper Gallery ..	"	3	" Staff-Serjeants of Out-pensioners.
21		"	4	"
22		"	6	"

J. WATSON,
Lieutenant and Quartermaster.

(U.)

ROYAL HOSPITAL, KILMAINHAM.

RETURN of In-Pensioners of the above Establishment who are in the possession of Medals for
"War Services."

October, 1870.

Name of Actions, &c.	Number.	Remarks.
Peninsula and Waterloo ..	18	
Waterloo	2	
Bhurtpore	8	
Burmah	6	
Salade	9	
Scinde	2	
South Africa	7	
Crimea	18	} Private Donoghue, late 9th Lancers, has also the Victoria Cross.
Indian Mutiny	7	
New Zealand	6	
Total ..	**80**	

WM. McGILL, Captain,
Adjutant, Royal Hospital.

(V.)

ROYAL HOSPITAL, KILMAINHAM.

RETURN of the Number of In-Pensioners who have lost a Leg or an Arm, at the Ages
specified below.

October 1870.

Ages.	Lost a Leg.	Lost an Arm.	Remarks.
Between 30 and 40	..	..	
„ 40 „ 50	..	..	
„ 50 „ 60	..	..	
„ 60 „ 70	8	3	
Total	**8**	**1**	

WM. McGILL, Captain,
Adjutant, Royal Hospital.

(W.)

STATEMENT showing the Total Actual Expenditure on the Royal Hospital, Kilmainham, from 1856-57 to 1869-70.

Average Cost per Annum — — — — — — L.sX. s. d.
* When joined this Expenditure has been provided for by Board of Works.
† The Expenditure has been provided for by the Bank of Works.

G. F. DUNN, Secretary.

(X.)

STATEMENT showing the Actual Cost to the Public of the In-Pensioners of the Royal Hospital, Kilmainham, from 1856-57 to 1869-70.

Actual Annual Average Cost of In-Pensioner Establishment — — — — — — L.s.d.
Actual Annual Average Cost of an In-Pensioner — — — — — — L.s.d.

G. F. DUNN, Secretary.

o

(Y.)

MEMORANDUM relative to the Lands of the Royal Hospital, Kilmainham.

				A.	R.	P.
Under Main Building and Grounds	..	..	..	5	3	57
Under Infirmary and Grounds, Gardens and Laundry	..	..	3	1	12
Military Road Field	..	..	..	..	0	1	3
Western Avenue	..	..	..	..	1	3	31
Burial ground	..	..	..	..	0	0	6
" Bully's Acre "	..	..	..	..	1	0	33
Master's Fields	..	..	..	..	11	1	20
Deputy-Master's Field	..	..	..	3	0	6
Master's Garden	..	..	..	..	0	1	70
Deputy-Master's Garden	..	..	..	0	1	34
New Stables	..	..	..	..	0	3	0
Island Bridge Barracks	..	..	..	1	1	0
Conveyed to Great Southern and Western Railway	..	..	21	3	5½
				60	**3**	**57**

The Military road, the two roads leading to Island Bridge, a piece of ground which adjoined " Bully's Acre," and a piece cut off in making the Circular Road, make up the 64 acres granted by the Charter.

G. F. DUNN,
Secretary and Treasurer.

(Z.)

RETURN showing the numbers in the Royal Hospital, Kilmainham, on the 1st January in each year.

Year.	Numbers.	Vacancies.
1856	199	4
1857	194	6
1858	139	5
1859	139	1
1860	139	0
1861	140	..
1862	140	..
1863	140	..
1864	140	..
1865	140	..
1866	140	..
1867	140	..
1868	140	..
1869	140	..
1870	140	..

G. F. DUNN,
Secretary and Treasurer.

(AA.)

ROYAL HOSPITAL, KILMAINHAM.

RETURN of Pensioners fit for Hospital Duty at the Ages specified below.

Ages.	Staff Sergeant.	Sergeants.	Corporals.	Acting Corporals.	Drummer.	Privates.	Total.	Employed.	Remarks.
Between 30 and 40	..	..	..	..	..	..	..	..	
" 40 and 50	..	1	1	1	..	22	25	1	
" 50 and 60	..	1	1	1	1	16	20	2	
" 60 and 70	..	1	2	2	..	6	9	1	
Total	..	3	4	4	1	44	56	6	

WM. McGILL, Captain,
Adjutant, Royal Hospital.

(BB.)

REPORT showing the present cost of Clothing and Food of an In-Pensioner of the Royal Hospital, Kilmainham, and particulars of Lodging, Bedding, &c., &c.

	£	s.	d.
Annual cost under present contract, of clothing supplied to an In-Pensioner	4	6	6
The annual cost for a Staff Serjeant in Serjeant	7	17	11
(For particulars of clothing, see a)	4	3	3
The annual cost of rations, including porter, is per annum	19	11	6
(For particulars of rations, see b)			
(For particulars of lodgings, &c., see c.)			

J. WATSON,
Lieutenant and Quartermaster.

(a.)

Particulars of Clothing.

The contract for clothing is made for 3 years, and each man receives—

1st Year.
1 blue coat, to last 3 years.
1 red coat, to last 3 years.
1 blue jacket, to last 3 years.
1 pair of trousers.
2 pairs of blucher boots.
3 cotton shirts.
3 flannel vests.

2 pairs of cotton web drawers.
2 pairs of woollen socks.
3 linen collars.
2 night caps.
2 pocket handkerchiefs.
1 hair brush.
1 hair comb.

2nd Year.
1 pair of trousers.
2 pairs of blucher boots.
3 cotton shirts.
3 flannel vests.
2 pairs of woollen socks.
2 pairs of cotton web drawers.
2 night caps.

3 linen collars.
2 pocket handkerchiefs.
1 pair of braces, to last for 2 years.
1 forage cap, to last for 3 years.
1 pairs of boots, to last for 3 years.
1 hair brush.
1 hair comb.

3rd Year. 1 red coat, to last 3 years (3 years under next contract).
1 blue jacket, to last 3 years.
1 pair of trousers.
2 pairs of blucher boots.
3 cotton shirts.
3 flannel vests.

2 pairs of web cotton drawers.
2 pairs of socks.
2 night caps.
3 linen collars.
2 cotton pocket handkerchiefs.
1 hair brush.
1 hair comb.

The cushel hose and leather stocks are issued only when required; the last issue of the former was on 1st January, 1863, of the latter on the 1st January, 1861.

THE cost of the Clothing under the present Contract.

			For a Staff Serjeant.			For a Serjeant.			For a Private.		
			£	s.	d.	£	s.	d.	£	s.	d.
First year			7	19	5	7	3	4	5	6	6
Second year			7	13	11	5	11	9	5	5	4
Third year			7	18	5	5	11	0	4	7	6
Total for the 3 years			23	10	9	16	3	4	15	19	6

(b.)

Particulars of Rations.

For Man on Wednesdays, Mondays, Thursdays, and Saturdays.

a loaf of bread weighing				1½ pound.
butter				1 ounce.
good black tea				
good moist sugar				
the best new milk				¼ pint.
beef (leg and round), without bone				16 ounces.
porter				½ pint.
soup				1

Q 2

For Men on Sundays and Tuesdays.	a loaf of bread weighing	..	..	..	..	..	1½ pound.
	butter	..	..	..	..	..	1 ounce.
	good black tea	..	..	..	..	..	
	good moist sugar	..	..	..	..	..	2
	the best new milk	..	..	..	..	..	1 pint.
	mutton, baked	..	..	..	..	..	13 ounces.
	potatoes	..	..	..	..	..	1 pound.
	porter	..	..	..	..	..	1 pint.
For Men on Fridays.	a loaf of bread weighing	..	..	..	..	..	1 pound.
	butter	..	..	..	..	..	1 ounce.
	haddock, in lieu of meat	..	..	..	..	..	1
	good black tea	..	..	..	..	..	
	good moist sugar	..	..	..	..	..	2
	the best new milk	..	..	..	..	..	
	porter	..	..	..	..	..	1 pint.

A sufficient quantity of herbs, oatmeal, salt, and pepper is supplied.

A double ration is allowed to each man on the anniversary of Her Majesty's Birthday, Christmas, and St. Patrick's days.

Articles washed weekly for each man:—

2 cotton shirts.	1 pair of drawers.
2 pairs of socks.	1 night cap.
2 towels.	1 pocket-handkerchief.
1 flannel vest.	

1 pair of sheets for tents,
the linen mattress covers when necessary.

The cost of washing is 6½d. per week per man, or 1l. 8s. 10d. per annum.

(c.)

Particulars of Lodging, Bedding, &c.

Each room accommodates 5 men, and is fitted with—

iron shelves.	1 tin of blacking, 3 shoe brushes.
1 small coal box.	1 cloth brush.
1 fender, 1 set of fire-irons.	1 table, 5 chairs.
1 water can, 1 washhand basin.	1 tea kettle, 1 saucepan, 1 frying pan.
1 foot bath.	1 coalsifter, 1 soap tray.
1 slop pail, 1 mop, 1 hair broom.	1 gas light.
1 hearth brush, 1 pair of bellows.	5 iron bedsteads.

And each man is supplied with the following:—

1 screw pallaisse.	1 quilt.
1 hair mattress.	1 knife, fork, and spoon.
1 linen cover for ditto.	1 mess tin with centre piece.
1 hair bolster.	2 pewter tins.
3 linen covers for ditto.	2 towels.
3 pairs of blankets.	1 piece of soap.
2 pairs of sheets.	1 pewter pot.

There are also provided for general use in the Hall, &c.—

Tables, forms, open with hooks, settles, and cross-chairs, porter, tea, and soup cans, tureens, dishes, and plates, carving knives and forks.

Bath with hot and cold water. Copper optimums and tubics for games, such as backgammon, draughts, &c.

(DD.)

ROYAL HOSPITAL, KILMAINHAM.

CLASSIFICATION of In-Pensioners who require Medical Treatment.

Classification.	Number of Acute Diseases.	Number of Chronic Diseases.	Number of Debilitated Persons.	Total.	Classification.	Number requiring Comfort and Diet.	Number requiring Nothing.	Total.
In the Infirmary ..	6	99	5	110	In the Upper House..	45	34	79

WM. CARTE,
Physician and Surgeon, Royal Hospital.

(EE.)

ROYAL HOSPITAL, KILMAINHAM.

Number of Men in the Establishment suffering from the undermentioned diseases.

Paralysis.	Ruptures.	Urinary Affections.	Old Age and Debility.	Total.
19	13	24	65	116

WM. CARTE,
Physician and Surgeon.

(FF.)

Minute by the Right Hon. Sir W. Mansfield, G.C.B., G.C.S.I., Commander of the Forces, and Master of Kilmainham Hospital.

I HAVE been so short a time in the office of Master at the Royal Hospital, Kilmainham, that I am unable to offer reliable information on the working of the details, but it seems to me that in an Institution of the kind two principles should be steadily had in view, viz.,—

To give the fullest development to the charity and the use of the buildings and other advantages, and to keep down the working Staff to what is actually required.

I give in the margin a list of the working Staff of the Hospital, it being understood that this is only a Staff for the execution of orders, and that the real responsibility for the Establishment rests with the Master and the Board of Governors. It appears to me that taking these facts into consideration the Staff is larger than is necessary, while I do not understand why the number of Pensioners accommodated at Kilmainham should be so restricted. Applications sometimes come for vacancies in the Hospital, and if I may judge from the appeals of those who have been expelled for misconduct, it is clear that the position of an In-Pensioner at Kilmainham is much prized; when to this it is added that there are many hundreds of Out-Pensioners in Ireland whose age exceeds 60 years, and to whom therefore a refuge in the Hospital could not fail to be an important boon, I confess that I should like to see the numbers extended, the room now taken up by a redundant Staff, and by Offices, as I am informed, for the payment of Out-Pensioners, being applied to the purpose.

It seems to me that the Staff might properly consist of an Adjutant and Quartermaster, a Surgeon, a Chaplain.

I fail to see what a Civil Secretary can have to do, which could not be done by the Adjutant, seeing that there are no Regimental duties of drill, &c., as in a body of soldiers.

I am given to understand, but I do not speak from any exact data, that the Institution of the Royal Hospital is one that is prized by the community in Dublin, and that its abolition would be received most unwillingly.

Although it would be impossible to house all the Out-Pensioners of a large Army, nevertheless it does appear to me very advantageous to have such an Institution as Kilmainham in the Capital of Ireland, which may be the resort of a few old worn out soldiers, or of men who have lost their limbs in the service of their country.

I believe the moral and political good performed by such Institutions far to exceed the physical comfort bestowed by them on a few individuals.

In the discussions which took place from 30 to 40 years ago on this subject, this point was overlooked by all except the late Sir H. Vivian, the Secretary at War having convinced himself that the individuals affected comprised the whole matter under consideration.

Accordingly he argued that if he bribed all the men out of the Institution by a small addition to their pensions, there was no injustice done, and the late Sir Hussey Vivian had no cause of complaint.

As above suggested, the view appears a very narrow one, which will not bear the test of even superficial examination.

The Hospital having been established as a means of charity to old servants of the State no longer able to take care of themselves, it is evident that its object has not altogether failed, if it be necessary to bribe the Pensioners to leave it; that is to say, that a very small portion of the Pensioners of the Army are, as a consequence of this charity, better off than the Out-Pensioners.

In getting rid of the charity, which, after all, was originally endowed by Army subscriptions, the Secretary at War in 1833, while professing to be just, and even generous, to the individuals immediately concerned, was clearly unjust to the successors of those individuals, as represented by the small section of Pensioners at large, which would otherwise have been fortunate enough to find a refuge in the Hospital. I may unjust with regard to the original intention of the founder and to the subscriptions by which the Hospital was maintained until Parliament assumed charge. But there is a point to consider which has a large application beyond the walls of the Hospital. Then, if the In-Pensioners be discharged from the Hospital with an addition to their pensions, they will be placed in a better position than their comrades, who have always been Out-Pensioners. The latter will have a right to enquire why, having done the same service to the State, they are to receive a less pension than the men coming out of Kilmainham, and further, the question might be raised by the Public at large whether the whole system of pensions for retired soldiers did not call for increase. In these days it would not be difficult to raise such a cry, and I cannot but think that the attempt to bribe men to leave the Hospital and to become Out-Pensioners would be a fair ground for proceedings in such a cause.

W. R. MANSFIELD, Lieutenant-General,
Commanding the Forces in Ireland.

Royal Hospital, Dublin,
October 22nd, 1870.

(GG.)

ABSTRACT of Statements made by certain In-Pensioners of the Royal Hospital at Kilmainham, in answer to questions put to them by the Chairman of the Committee, on Saturday, 22nd October, 1870.

Thomas White, late 50th Regiment.

Out-pension, 9d.; has no family; would rather remain in the Hospital than go out with 1s. 6d. a-day.

Martin Allen, late 30th Regiment.

Out-pension 8d.; has no wife or family; would rather go out of the Hospital if he had 1s. 6d. a-day; could do with less rations than he has in the Hospital.

Thomas Butler, late 7th Fusiliers.

Out-pension 6d.; has been three years in the Hospital; nine years' service; has children, but no wife; would sooner have 1s. 6d. a-day and go out of the Hospital, because he would like to live with his children. If he had not a family he would rather stop in the Hospital; has no complaint to make whatever; no one could be better treated; has no complaint to make of the discipline of the Hospital.

John Kelly, late 48th Regiment.

Out-pension 1s.; has been in the Hospital since last February; if he had been able to work would not have applied to come into the Hospital; finds the Hospital to be a different place to what he thought it was before coming in; if he had known what sort of a place it was he would have applied to come in sooner. A man in the Hospital is in his opinion better off than he would be with 1s. a-day outside; had no complaint to make of the discipline; plenty of library is allowed; has no family, and would prefer staying in the Hospital to going out with 1s. 6d. a-day.

James Connor, late 34th Regiment.

Out-pension 8d.; was discharged in 1859; came into the Hospital in 1867; not married; would rather remain in the Hospital with the comforts that he gets there than have 1s. 6d. a-day and go out. In his state of health 1s. 6d. would be no good to him; he might have to go into a Hospital.

William Wilkinson, late 94th Regiment.

A Scotchman, aged 63; out-pension 8d.; came into the Hospital in 1865; stayed out till he could work no longer; has no wife or family; is very comfortable in the Hospital; the best men in Dublin could not be better treated; would rather remain in the Hospital than go out with even 3s. a-day; has no complaint to make of the discipline; it is very hard to get leave.

William Tennant, late 99th Regiment.

Out-pension 8d.; married; came into the Hospital in 1845, three years after he was married; sweeps out the corridor; his wife lives in Dublin and does work for the officers in the house; came into the Hospital because he had such a low pension outside, and could not do much work on account of having a bad leg; allowed to take rations to his wife and takes them to her; finds no inconvenience in being separated from his wife; can get leave any night by asking for it. The rations are scarcely enough to feed himself and his wife, but he cannot eat all she brings allowed him; does not know whether any of those who have not wives sell their rations; they may do so; he is not supposed to know. He would sooner go out of the Hospital and have 1s. 6d. a-day, for the sake of his wife; if he were a single man he would rather remain in, than have 1s. 6d. a-day and go out.

Peter Fitzpatrick, late 4th Dragoons.

Out-pension 8d.; has been in the Hospital nine years; married since he came in; his wife comes to see him in the Hospital and he goes out to see her; gives her any money he can afford. Is gardener to Mr. Hare, so that he can eat all his rations. If he cannot eat all his bread he gives it to his wife; would prefer staying in the Hospital to going outside and having 1s. 6d. a-day.

Richard Hughes, late 1st Royals.

Aged 77; has been in the Hospital eleven years; has no wife, but has two children who support themselves; would sooner stay in the Hospital than have 1s. 6d. a-day and go out.

In-Pensioners in the Infirmary.

W. Smith, late 32nd Regiment.

Age 66; out-pension 1d.; is very comfortable in every way, and 10s. a-day would not compensate him for the benefits he receives.

J Pearce, late 23rd Foot.

Age 49; out-pension 11d.; is very comfortable and "hopes the Government won't break "the Home up."

J. Walsh, late 45th Foot.

Age 43; out-pension 8d.; is very comfortable, and 8s. a-day would not recompense him for what he gets in the Hospital.

W. Keating, 97th Foot.

Age 51; out-pension 8d.; is very comfortable and 8s. a-day would not compensate him.

J. Leary, late 80th Regiment.

Age 70; out-pension 8d.; is a cripple, owing to an injury to one of his legs. "The comfort " of the Home is more to him than any increase " of pension would be."

F. Solon, late 3rd Dragoon Guards.

Age 75; out-pension 9d.; is very comfortable, and has no wish to leave the Hospital.

Warrant, ordering that when Officers surrender their Commissions, the Buyer and Seller shall each pay twelve pence to the person to the use of the Royal Hospital at Chelsea, 17th March, 168¾.

G. R.

Whereas, out of Our great care for the maintenance of such as have, or shall have served in Our Land Forces, We have given order for the building and finishing a Royal Hospital; and it being also reasonable that such Officers as receive Our Commissions should contribute to so good and charitable a work. Our Will and Pleasure is, that when any Governor of Our Forts or Garrisons, or any Commission Officer of Our Land Forces, shall obtain leave from us to surrender his Commission, Command, or Employment, and that at his humble request We shall grant the same to any other. That in such case the person to surrendering his Command shall pay twelve pence out of every twenty shillings that shall be given him in case of such surrender. And that the person likewise to whom the said surrender shall be made, shall also pay twelve pence for every twenty shillings given to the person surrendering as aforesaid; and to the end a true account may be had of the money so appointed by Us to be reserved for the use of Our said Hospital. We do further direct, that no Commission be issued out of the Office of either of Our Principal Secretaries of State, to any Governor or Officer of Our said Forts, Garrisons, or Land Forces, without a certificate first had from the Paymaster-General of Our Forces, that such persons to surrendering, to whose behoof such surrender is made, shall have each of them duly satisfied the said reservation of twelve pence out of every twenty shillings, or given sufficient security for payment of the same to Our said Paymaster for the use of Our said Royal Hospital. And We do further charge and command the said Paymaster of Our Forces to take care, upon the application of such person, as aforesaid, that such Certificate be duly given, so soon as they shall appear to have complied with Our Will and Pleasure.

Given at our Court at Newmarket, the 17th day of March, 168¾, in the 35th year of our Reign.

By His Majesty's Command.

(I L.)

Cholera Out-Pensioners in Districts in Ireland.

Abstract of Returns obtained from Staff Officers of Pensioners in Ireland, at the request of the Committee.

Districts.	Number of Pensioners in Workhouses	Number between 20 and 40 years of age.	Number who are 60 years of age and upwards.	Number who have been rendered incapable of maintaining their Pensions by labour in consequence of wounds or other disabilities contracted in and by the Service.
Armagh	1	272	226	164
Athlone	1	319	229	83
Ballymena	1	247	217	100
Belfast, &c.	1	168	282	76
Birr			210	
Carlow			127	
Cavan	7		123	
Clonmel			162	
Cork, No. 1			162	
" No. 2	NIL.		148	
Dublin, No. 1	7		214	
" No. 2			267	
Ennis	NIL.		264	
Enniskillen	NIL.		154	
Galway			162	
Kilkenny	6		167	
Limerick	2		165	
Londonderry	270.		174	
Longford	4		123	
Kerry	NIL.		160	
Omagh	1		148	
Sligo	2		126	
Tralee			177	
Tullamore	4		114	
Waterford	1	132	71	
Total	70	1,349	4,923	1,045

War Office,
January, 1871.